THE
FARTER'S
SURVIVAL
GUIDE

Other books by the author:

The Art of the Fart

The Great British Fart-Off

The Official Fartway Code

I Can Make You Fart

The Bottomologicon (with Whiffles McSpudge)

The Joy of Farting

How to Avoid Huge Farts

Eats, Farts and Leaves: A Vegetarian Cookbook

THE
FARTER'S
Survival
Guide

BENET DONALD

Illustrated by Tom Wharton

Michael O'Mara Books Limited

I would like to dedicate this utterly silly book to Scotty, Ash, Yasmin, Lawrence, Phil, Chris, Brydie, Jamie, Casey and everyone at the Swan. You guys are so bloody nice.

The acknowledgements on page 185 are obviously total bullshit, but I would genuinely like to thank Jon Elek, Hugh Barker, George Maudsley and Jo Stansall. And many congratulations and all my love to Tom and Sneha.

First published in Great Britain in 2015 by
Michael O'Mara Books Limited
9 Lion Yard
Tremadoc Road
London SW4 7NQ

A CIP catalogue record for this book is available from the British Library.

Papers used by Michael O'Mara Books Limited are natural, recyclable products made from wood grown in sustainable forests. The manufacturing processes conform to the environmental regulations of the country of origin.

ISBN: 978-1-78243-460-3 in paperback print format

1 3 5 7 9 10 8 6 4 2

Designed and typeset by Design 23
Illustrations by Tom Wharton

Printed and bound by CPI Group (UK) Ltd, Croydon CR0 4YY

www.mombooks.com

CONTENTS

INTRODUCTION

Farting isn't entirely dissimilar to writing about farting: a furtive, lonely exercise that one guiltily enjoys but about which, if someone else did it, one would protest in the strongest possible terms. Certainly when I was first asked to write a book about farting I spent a while in a dark room thinking long and hard about the life decisions that had brought me to this point. But it doesn't do to wallow, and when I had cheerfully come to terms with my fate I realized that *The Farter's Survival Guide* could be a genuinely helpful book.

In reality, there are really only three routes that can be taken by the farting survivalist: the safe route (apologize or make good), the riskier approach (run away) and the kamikaze option (blame someone else or do something equally chaotic). This doesn't mean, however, that there aren't a hell of a lot of different ways you can explore these solutions in a variety of scenarios. In this very informative guide you will find a mixture of ordinary farting scenarios (a crowded lift; a wedding) and somewhat more exotic ones (while performing a striptease; being abducted by aliens). As the reader you can decide, based on the character's choices up to the moment they fart, which option out of the three you are going to choose. Ideally, you will steer the majority of your protagonists to deliverance from social suicide. The hope is that by observing the various outcomes, you will know what to do if you find yourself in a similar situation.

Nestled amongst these scenarios you will also find two fartventures, in which you must journey through a sequence of terrifying choices after accidentally doing a colossal blow-off. The odds are against you. Good luck! There are also twenty Big Trump playing cards, which you can photocopy (or cut out, frankly – I won't stop you) and play against each other. These are a selection of society's highest-risk and most vicious farters, beautifully illustrated by Tom Wharton (who seems able effortlessly to reveal their essential seediness). You must pit yourself against other players to see who comes out on top as the farting supremo.

And finally, if you're not reading this while on the toilet, well then thank you. I really appreciate one person reading it while not . . . now wait, where are you going . . . oh *fine*. Do your damn business. In fairness, if I could have conveniently written this while sat on the toilet then for verisimilitude's sake I would have done, but I am pleased to report moderate and regular movements that require only a brief daily visit, meaning my villainous editor (see scenario 12) would have been kept waiting years for delivery of the manuscript.

Toot toot!

Benet Donald

SCENARIOS
1–6

(BEGINNERS)

SURVIVAL SCENARIO 1: THE WEDDING

It is **Subject S**'s wedding day. It should be the happiest day of her life but all she can tell herself is: soon it will be over. She hasn't slept properly for a fortnight and feels like she's been through some sort of boot camp. There should be a military medal for putting up with this much advice from your mother.

After a few last fussing ministrations from her beautician cousin Maggie outside the door, **Subject S** is inside the church. The little old organist spots her and starts playing. And there he is. Dear **Dan**. She has never been happier to see anyone in her whole life. In what feels like a moment she's at the altar and just a few minutes later (she refused to have a full mass – give them an inch and they'll start reading out things about lepers and tax collectors) they're at the vows.

Dan: I do solemnly declare . . .

Now she is ready to well up. It is at this moment, however, that she is blindsided by the nastiest fart of her entire life. Nerves have been bubbling in her empty stomach since four thirty this morning, when she awoke. She must have been dimly aware of the need to go to the toilet, but it was simply too low on her long list of priorities. And what has come out is one so intense and concentrated, it's made of pure evil.

She goes rigid and stares at **Dan** in total terror. The dress is big and multi-layered, but even if it was made of asbestos it wouldn't keep him and the **Vicar** safe from this smell for long.

WHAT DOES SUBJECT S DO?

Solution A (Sane)

Well, she's not ruining the whole bloody day because of one unfortunate moment. Let's face it, if this is an aroma **Dan** really hasn't smelled before, he won't remain in that virgin state for long. Best get used to it now, buster. For better or worse, right? Right.

As for the **Vicar**, **Subject S** is truly sorry about him. He has the genial face of an old dog that sleeps by a pub fireplace. Later, in private, she will beg his forgiveness (which you would hope he would give, if he takes pride in his work). Anyhow, he must christen babies all the time, and they fart non-stop. *And* puke. He should count himself lucky she hasn't barfed all over his cassock.

As the odour reaches **Dan**, he goes stiff, just as she did. He stumbles on his words.

Dan: . . . you I wed, I mean, with this ring, er, I, I you wed . . .

Smile and wait, **Subject S** tells herself. Smile and wait. It *will* be over.

Dan's face muscles are twitching, his nostrils flaring into hoops. He can hardly talk. The congregation seem to be taking it for nerves and finding it incredibly sweet. The **Vicar**, on the other hand, is totally serene, watching him intently, without the slightest sign of discomfort. **Subject S** is silently awed by the **Vicar**'s self-control. What a pro, she thinks. What a *pro*!

Dan now places the ring on her finger. Suddenly, she realizes she's married. She looks up at **Dan** and the **Vicar**. They are both smiling.

Vicar: Repeat after me . . .

Solution B (Risky)

As **Dan** starts repeating the vows, **Subject S** raises a hand in front of his face. He stops.

She turns to the congregation.

Subject S: Okay. That was good. But not *great*. I'm going to come in again, and this time I want a bit more of an atmosphere, okay?

They stare back at her stupidly. She marches towards the back of the church, snapping her fingers at the bridesmaids to follow her.

Subject S: I want a *lot* more smiling. And maybe some clapping, too. This is an emotional occasion, right? I mean, are we made of stone? Let's give it some spunk! I'm going to come in on the count of three. YOU.

She points to the **Organist,** an elderly woman in a cardigan, with glasses almost as tall as her head, who has been stooping feebly over the keyboard.

Subject S: Can we spruce up the old wedding march a bit? Too trad. Maybe a bit more bluesy?

The **Organist** contemplates this for a moment, then shrugs acceptance.

Subject S: Okay. We're good to go. Come on folks, we can do this! Can I get a 'yeah'?

She receives in response a single, hesitant 'yeah?' from a boy in the middle of the crowd.

Subject S: I said CAN I GET A 'YEAH'?

She receives a positively loud 'yeah'.

Subject S: Okay! On the count of three. Hit it, you sexy bitch!

The **Organist** starts to play. No one can recall having smelled anything untoward.

Solution C (Kamikaze)

In one fluid movement, **Subject S** takes hold of the hem of her dress and whips it over her head, so that her frilly-knickered rear is facing the congregation. At lightning speed, she untucks the lighter that was hidden in the top of her stockings to facilitate the occasional cheeky fag on the big day, then holds it, with astonishing yogic suppleness, to her behind, igniting a blue belch of flame.

She straightens with the same graceful agility as before and then wags her eyebrows at her husband-to-be.

Subject S: Did I do it? Huh? Did I make it?

Dan nods dumbly.

Subject S: Woah! Thank you fans! First time!

She marches over to the nearest person in the congregation, an uncle who is in fact a recently retired
logistician for the Ministry of Transport.

Subject S: You lose, buddy! Ten pounds. Right now,
please.

Too bewildered to argue, he fishes a tenner from his
wallet and hands it over. **Subject S** hitches the skirt
of her dress up again and tucks the note in next to the
lighter.

Subject S (to the rest of the congregation): Sorry. I
CANNOT refuse a bet. Just can't do it. Never could.
Okay, let's do this. (Returns to her fiancé's side.) Where
were we?

Dan and the **Vicar** look at one another for a moment,
as though each is surprised to find the other still there.

Eventually their brains start working again, and they
start to speak:

Vicar: Repeat after me. I, Daniel James Finnigan . . .

Dan: Er, I, er . . . I, Daniel James . . . Finnigan . . .

SURVIVAL SCENARIO 2:
THE LIBRARY

Monday afternoon in a sleepy public library. **Subject P**, a man of thirty, enters and enquires politely where the reference section is. The **Librarian**, a bespectacled lady of about sixty, points him to an empty room at the back of the building.

Subject P enters and selects a 1938 *Times Atlas*, which is roughly as tall as a two-man tent. He opens it on the table, then sits down and leans over it, snoozing.

He wakes up an hour later and releases the pint or so of pent-up post-lunch gas that has accumulated in his colon. That feels good, he thinks. Screw you, world.

Unfortunately, on this occasion, the world is one step ahead, and is thinking: screw you, **Subject P**. For he immediately discovers the **Librarian** is behind him, showing reference books to an **Old Man**.

Old Man: What was that?

Librarian: I didn't say anything.

WHAT DOES SUBJECT P DO?

Solution A (Sane)

Brief pre-smell phase

Subject P (peering over the **Librarian**'s shoulder): *A Pictorial History of Siberia*. Did you ever read Colin Thubron's travel book *In Siberia*? It's fascinating.

The **Old Man** and the **Librarian** mumble a response in the negative.

End of pre-smell phase

Subject P takes hold of their shoulders and physically hauls them across the room.

Subject P: It's over here, I think. You *must* read it. He draws fascinating parallels between the white people's treatment of the aboriginal Chukchi and Evenk tribes of Siberia and the plight of the Native Americans – not with respect, but as a people whose alcohol addiction must be serviced regularly, in order that they remain invisible to the rest of the 'regular' population. Sad and disgraceful, don't you think?

Old Man: Oh. Yes . . . perhaps . . .

Librarian (uncertainly): Quite fascinating . . .

Subject P pulls the book from the shelf and forces it into the **Old Man**'s hands. He then retires triumphantly back to his seat, where the smell has nearly dissipated.

Solution B (Risky)

Subject P jumps up and turns around, affronted.

Subject P: Was that you? That's disgusting! I come here, to a public place, in good faith, trusting that I shall not be molested by other people's anal outbursts.

Old Man: I'm not sure . . .

Subject P: To come *here*. A *library*. The final bastion of decency somehow clinging on despite the depredations of our small-minded government . . .

Librarian: I rather think . . .

Subject P: HERE. Where one's spirit can swell to encompass the wisdom of the ages . . . I see I was naive to seek solace in this place. I shall instead pass out of these doors and attempt to find an environment less aurally offensive. A sewer in Glasgow, perhaps, or the Black Hole of Kolkata. Good day.

Librarian: But I–

Subject P: GOOD DAY, MADAM.

Subject P storms out of the swing doors with his head held high.

Solution C (Kamikaze)

Subject P climbs onto his chair and turns around. He stoops and lets his arms swing beside his ankles, then climbs onto the table, making monkey noises.

Librarian: Get down from there at once!

Subject P licks his fingers, and glances stupidly around the room, his mouth agape, then starts tearing pages out of the *Times Atlas* and chewing them.

Old Man: Good lord, should I call the police?

Librarian: Oh dear. Excuse me! Have you got a carer who's nearby?

Subject P leaps up and wraps both hands around the flex of the light fitting, then dangles awkwardly before it rips clear of the ceiling and he crashes onto the floor with a scream of agonizing pain. He limps ape-like out of the room to the children's section, where he lowers his trousers and defecates in the kettle of a toddler's tea set.

The **Old Man** tends to the **Librarian**, who has fainted. Neither of them notice as **Subject P** saunters out, fully upright, cheerfully helping himself to a Malcolm Gladwell paperback on the way.

SURVIVAL SCENARIO 3: OPEN-HEART SURGERY

Subject G is a universally respected heart surgeon in his sixties. Today he is repairing the heart of an old woman. Usually he enjoys brusquely exerting his authority upon the lesser members of staff (which is everyone). However, joining him today is a visiting surgeon from Finland, an excruciatingly gorgeous woman thirty years his junior called **Karla**. She is even colder and more reserved than he usually is, which has had the effect of turning him (always nervous around beautiful women) positively garrulous.

At every juncture **Subject G** pauses to ask **Karla**'s opinion, then hurriedly agrees with her almost before she's finished. At one point he even bursts out laughing at something she said he thought was a joke, only realizing a moment later that, of course it *wouldn't* be a joke, because they're in the operating theatre. He can feel everyone staring at him.

Suddenly, he farts. A loud one.

WHAT DOES SUBJECT G DO?

Solution A (Safe)

Subject G (chuckling): Good lord, things have got very informal in operating theatres, haven't they?

Everyone is staring at him. They aren't sure where he's going with this. He reaches down to the surgical gown the patient is wearing and, lifting it up and then down, wafts it.

Subject G: Dear, oh dear. Stinky one. What are they putting in the hospital food? Nil by mouth, I thought I ordered. Tut, tut! (Chuckles again.)

Everyone has instinctively taken a step back from the operating table, surgical masks no doubt hiding their wrinkled noses. **Karla**, however, is clearly game.

Karla: Meatballs. With nutmeg.

Subject G (nodding, and pointing at the patient): Let's have no more from you, thank you, Mrs Stevenson!

Two of the nurses have started giggling and **Karla** is also shaking with laughter. In a few moments the operating theatre is the locus of a bout of mass hilarity, a group case of the giggles. The patient goes into cardiac arrest, but only briefly. They're still wiping the tears away as they watch the orderlies wheeling her out, and all agree to go for cocktails later.

Subject G is replete. He and **Karla** have a brief snog at around midnight before she throws up on his shoes. He gets a taxi home to his furious wife. Life is short. What fart?

Solution B (Risky)

When faced with the sound and imminent odour of his own fart, **Subject G** has to come to terms with several things:

1. He's never had sex with someone from Finland and is probably never going to.

2. The nurses in this hospital don't like him much. And for good reason. He's distant. Reserved. And a dick.

3. He's got another four years at this hospital before retirement. Relocating now would be a titanic arse-ache.

4. If news of this fart gets out he'll never live it down, and will have to endure years of being laughed at behind his back.

So he has to find a way out of this. He delves into the chest cavity to continue the operation, thinking hard. Then inspiration hits.

Subject G: I never expected to find this . . . How surprising!

He raises his hand slowly from the chest cavity and stares at it in confusion. Then, with a silky movement of his fingers, reveals he is holding a golf ball in his hands. It's a trick he learned to please his grandchildren, who otherwise find him a creepy bore. He does a cartoonish double-take at the golf ball.

Finding that he's still not quite getting the reception he expected, **Subject G** flings the golf ball over his shoulder. It bounces twice before landing neatly in the clear plastic bin for medical waste. The nurses aren't made of stone; they can acknowledge skill when they see it. They reward **Subject G** with a brief smattering of applause, while making mental notes about the professional complaint they'll be making about him later.

No one is thinking about the fart.

Solution C (Kamikaze)

Oh god. Farting in front of junior staff. Imagine what they'll make of it. It'll probably be the only thing he's ever remembered for. Not saving that six-year-old girl's life. Oh no. He'll just be remembered as old Mr Farty. Mr Stinkypants McStupidBum. Mr Farty Smelly Bumsmell.

Subject G is delving deep in the chest cavity, wrestling with these thoughts, when his hand starts to wriggle.

Subject G: *Argh!*

His hand shoots up, then pirouettes around, as though his wrist is a neck and his fingers evil eyes and smacking lips, surveying the whole room. The hand (which holds the scalpel) darts at him.

Subject G: It's possessed! Evil hand!

The hand then starts darting around the room trying to attack other people, like a Muppet crossed with *The Evil Dead*.

Subject G: Oh my god – leave them alone! Please, evil hand, what do you want? Is this because my house is built on top of an Indian burial ground? In *Raynes Park*?

The hand swivels to face him. It shakes itself, no.

Subject G: THEN WHY? Because you hate me. You *are* me. You want to destroy me! *Aaaaaaaaaaaargh!*

As the hand jabs the scalpel into his chest, **Subject G**'s screams curdle into bloody bubbles. Simultaneously, **Karla** smacks him over the back of the head with a bottle of oxygen, knocking him clean out. Everyone sighs with relief.

In the thousands of pages of paperwork that are filled out afterwards (the upshot of which is: detached retina; early retirement) no one makes a single mention of the fart.

WORDS OF WINDSDOM

'We are not amused. We are not! I insist it. Okay fine, that fart gag was quite funny. But I still don't believe in lesbians! If only Albert was here!'
QUEEN VICTORIA

SURVIVAL SCENARIO 4:
WHILE TICKET COLLECTING

Subject J is a ticket collector, making his way along a train. He is a ticket collector because he hates people. Look at them, he thinks, as he goes along. *He's* a pig. *She's* a pig. Look at *that* little pig, snuffling away on her packet of dried banana pieces. It is hatred (of all of them, except perhaps . . . no, all of them) that keeps him going.

Today, as **Subject J** walks along the moving train, he feels that welcome sense of power in his veins. Opening the door to a new carriage he sees a group of teenagers and starts to salivate. The mother lode. Middle-class teenagers, the best kind to terrorize. Smug, slouching, feet up on the seat, music blaring, hair stupid as you like. His natural prey. They'll be arrogant at first but in a few minutes he'll have them sitting in glum, possibly tearful silence.

Subject J: Tickets please.

Teen: Oh yeah mate, I'd like to get a single to Waterloo please.

Subject J allows the boy's words to hang in the air for a moment, his face registering nothing but lofty uninterest. This pause, during which the youngster will experience his first stirrings of doubt, is to **Subject J** like the first reverberating sting in a virtuoso guitar solo. The **Teen** is wonderfully posh, which will make this even more satisfying.

Subject J (laconically): Where did you get on the train?

But that's when he becomes aware of a disturbance in his bottom area. It's his worst nightmare come true. He has let off a big stinker.

WHAT DOES SUBJECT J DO?

Solution A (Safe)

Within two seconds each of the teens has caught wind of the awful guff. They're already making incredulous high-pitched screams and pointing at **Subject J**. The tables have turned – now it's like *their* Christmasses have all come at once. They jump up and run through the door into the next carriage. The other customers are also starting to stir as well. It really is an unpleasant aroma. **Subject J** just stands there. Two stations come and go; no one gets on.

Subject J remembers an uncle who used to visit, who had a particularly argumentative wife. She never gave him any peace, would ridicule him and everything he said, even in company. But his uncle would just sit there like Buddha, smiling, pretending blissful ignorance as though he was stone deaf. **Subject J** has suddenly realized that there is a

27

beauty and simplicity in this approach to life's problems. So he sits down.

Subject J remains motionless, watching suburbia trundle past him, enjoying a rare tranquil moment from this life. The sky is a peaceful, innocent blue. Perhaps he shouldn't be so spiteful towards young people after all.

But then he thinks: fuck it. They are *all* shitheads.

Solution B (Risky)

Subject J doesn't bat an eyelid. He regularly works on services that go past the sewage works at Berrylands just outside Surbiton, a smell so vile it causes polite strangers to stare askance at each other in presumed guilt. So before a second has passed he knows what to do.

Subject J: Don't overreact to the smell, just the sewage works. Show me your tickets.

Easy as that. Reassurance that the smell comes from a few thousand anonymous people (as opposed to the arsehole directly in front of their faces) is coupled with the fear of imminent arrest and prosecution for not having a ticket. Together these factors entirely overcome the teens' discomfort of smelling bum gas.

In fact, the memory of the fart smell, plus the shame and humiliation of the experience, all fuse together to form a sort of psychic knot of discomfort in each of them. Afterwards, the very thought of doing wrong causes the teenagers stomach-churning physical anguish, which leads them into a new life of moral rectitude, rejecting the arrogant ways of youth. Later they are to form a new political party based on mutual respect. They sweep to power in a grand clearing-out of the old order in the election of 2025. Britain prospers harmoniously for a thousand years.

Solution C (Kamikaze)

Subject J happened to catch one of the recent Batman movies on the TV last night. He grabs the nearest teen by the expensively tailored scruff of his preppy shirt, pulls him close and attempts a voice like Christian Bale's gravely growl.

Subject J: You know what I call you guys?

Teen: Wh-what?

Subject J: PUNKS. You know what punks are?

Teen: N—

Subject J (grabbing the second teen with his spare hand): Punks are a disease. *You know what I am?*

Second Teen: You're mental, mate!

First Teen: I think I know!

Subject J swivels his head towards the first teen without moving his shoulders, like he imagines Christian Bale would do. The movement sends an agonizing pain through his neck, giving his performance a new intensity.

First Teen: I've got a pretty fair idea what you were going to say. You were going to say, er, that you are, er, the cure.

Subject J: Correct. Consider yourself cured.

As the train pulls in, the doors open and he tosses both teens out onto the platform.

Subject J: Next time buy a ticket, you little punks. Lesson over.

The doors close right in front of **Subject J**'s face (luckily just missing the tip of his nose, which would have ruined the effect entirely). He stays perfectly still and maintains eye contact with the teens as the train moves out of the station. Then he turns to the other customers on the train (none of whom can remember detecting a fart smell) and says in his normal, squeaky voice, 'Tickets please . . .'

SURVIVAL SCENARIO 5: THE YOGA LESSON

Subject E isn't the sort of guy who'd usually be in a yoga class. Or any sort of class, except the selfish, unhealthy, drinker's and smoker's class. But over the last eighteen months all the drinking and kebabs have caught up with his thirty-seven-year-old frame and he's more overweight than he's comfortable with. So here he is, on time and dressed in kit that is cleanish for him, about to hunker down among a bunch of adults who are, without exception, physically . . . well, gorgeous. Not usually burdened with self-consciousness, **Subject E** cannot help feeling that he is a grubby little badger among shining peacocks.

The beautiful, pristinely controlled forty-five-year-old **Instructor** invites them to lie flat and then using just words proceeds to stretch and then curl this group of super-beings into a multitude of seemingly impossible positions. It's like bloody human origami.

Subject E does it too. But he breaks wind at the same time. And not silently. It makes a noise like someone dragging a dresser over a stone floor, or an angry mute let loose on a tuba. Unfortunately it's not in **Subject E**'s power to spontaneously combust, which is what he would ideally like to do right now. He's stuck here.

WHAT DOES SUBJECT E DO?

Solution A (Safe)

All of us – Winston Churchill, Abraham Lincoln, Buddha – we've all wanted to blame someone else for a fart. It's natural, it's human. And now **Subject E** gives right the hell into that temptation.

Subject E turns to the bloke behind him. He's sculpted, beautiful, angular, loathsome. His legs and visible chest area are not covered, like **Subject E**'s, by a thatch of untamed gorse, but sheened by a whisper of gold silken down. **Subject E** almost feels bad about playing the blame game but hey, it's a downward-facing-dog-eat-dog world we're living in, bro. Best get used to it.

Subject E (very loudly and aggressively): Excuse me, would you mind keeping control of your guts? Thank you.

Subject E continues practising his exercises with what he hopes is an appearance of indignation and disgust. The recipient of his opprobrium continues his yoga moves with perfect poise. He is either deaf, or has bulletproof self-esteem.

Everyone else in the room remains silent and disciplined. **Subject E** has no way of telling if his ruse has worked. A reasonable person, he therefore assumes it has failed and spends the rest of the hour-long session planning a new life for himself. He will get a new job, move to another part of the country (or possibly another country entirely) and never return to this city. Under any circumstances. Ever.

Solution B (Risky)

Subject E is right in the middle of the room. He can't get up and just run out – he has been doing the downward facing dog and the blood has rushed to his head. If he ran he'd just career across the place and smash into people. He does a quick scan of the room to make sure he doesn't know anyone here.

Subject E: I done a funny smell!

He says this in a cheerful, sing-song sort of way. The message to the rest of the room is unmistakable. The **Instructor** looks caught in the headlights.

Subject E: Are you my mummy?

Instructor: Er . . . no.

Subject E: Okay, Mummy.

For the rest of the session **Subject E** maintains a bright smile, which he turns into a manic grin if he catches anyone's eye. He also makes a point of breaking wind whenever the inclination arises, just to stay in character.

Two weeks later **Subject E** is taking an evening stroll with his girlfriend when he sees the **Instructor** crossing the road in front of him. **Subject E** screams, runs and vaults the nearby railings, disappearing into the park. He returns home later that night, forever afterward refusing to explain his actions.

Solution C (Kamikaze)

Subject E (leaping to his feet and speaking in a brisk,

helpful voice): So, do you want to know where you went wrong?

Instructor: I beg your pardon?

Subject E: Yoga inspector. The name's Shambo Spunce. This is a spot-check.

He stands in the middle of the class, arms akimbo, surrounded by his own gas. He looks around the room and nods appreciatively.

Subject E: Nice decor. Good light. Floor could do with a bit of a polish . . .

Instructor: I'm . . . I'm in the middle of a lesson.

Subject E (walking to the front of the room): Hmm. Your manner could do with some improvement. Chippy, we call it, in the yoga-inspecting trade. You might want to watch that.

The **Instructor** has passed very quickly through a series of strong conflicting emotions, whose ferocity now starts to ebb. Now she eyes him with a certain *froideur*.

Instructor: You're *so* not a yoga inspector.

Subject E: Sure I am. Here's my ID. (Fumbles in his pocket.) Oh. Well, it must be in my other shorts.

Jethrun Tangle and Susan Horp-Horp-Harp here are my assistants, they can confirm my credentials.

He gestures to a guy and a girl near the front of the class. They are both concentrating on remaining balanced with their left legs extended high into the air, and don't even realize they're being spoken to.

Subject E: Of course, I shouldn't address them directly. They're deep undercover.

Instructor: I'm calling security. Okay everyone, you can relax your pose. I'm sorry about this . . .

She exits. Once she's gone **Subject E** shambles over to leave.

Subject E: Decent door. I'd give it a . . . two point four out of five . . . Make a note of that, Jethrun!

Subject E then walks out, ignoring the mixture of furious and frightened glances he is receiving. He wonders briefly if he went a bit far with the name Horp-Horp-Harp. He hides in the showers until he thinks it's safe to sneak out of the building, and is then ignominiously wrestled to the floor by security as he tries to slip out through the turnstiles. He is photographed and formally banned from ever entering any of the company's 257 gyms again. No one makes any mention of a fart, though.

SURVIVAL SCENARIO 6:
WHILE SELLING A HOUSE

Subject L is a young estate agent and is therefore both wonderfully unintelligent and patronising. He is taking a young couple around a small house in suburbia. The couple, **Gary** and **Jane**, seem pleasant and honest – humble even – and therefore **Subject L** instinctively dislikes and distrusts them. The house is, naturally, unpleasant and he has every intention of bullying them into offering on it. He has a feeling that if pressed, they will do so simply to avoid a scene. They are currently standing in a room barely larger than a coffin. **Subject L** is talking up the room from the corridor outside, as the room can't hold all three of them.

Subject L: This is the second bedroom.

Gary and Jane: *Oh*.

Subject L: Lovely view of the garden.

Gary bangs his head on the angle of the wall as he fails to catch a glimpse of the promised view. **Subject L** sighs and looks at his watch, clicks his teeth and descends the staircase.

Subject L is the sort of person who thinks getting an egg and cheeseburger for breakfast 'on the go' is not only acceptable but the action of a fleet-footed go-getter. Armed with this knowledge, we need not be surprised when he lets fly with a deep rumbling grunt, right there on the stairs. A fog of foul-smelling gas rises to his nostrils. And **Gary** and **Jane** are about to descend right into it.

WHAT DOES SUBJECT L DO?

Solution A (Sane)

Subject L doesn't miss a beat. Before they've even reached the top of the stairs he's got a plan:

Subject L: Some of these old houses . . .

He pauses as the smell hits their nostrils, and **Gary** and **Jane** rear away from it in horror.

Subject L: . . . can have some funny aromas.

Jane (clutching her nose): Ugh!

Subject L (smiling ruefully): Well, it's to be expected, of course. When it's not been lived in for this long.

Gary and **Jane** are both staring at him in disbelief. They know the smell is his. He knows that they do. And they know that he knows it. As an estate agent, however, he does not belong to our reality, but to one in which everything he says is the saintly truth. Therefore he elects not to notice their stares of disdain and, wandering into the unsightly downstairs bathroom, begins to point out its non-existent positives. **Gary** and **Jane** are powerless to do anything but follow. In a way, they admire him as much as they are disgusted by him. Together these emotions coagulate into a sort of fear: this battle of wills is over. **Subject L** has won. The smell is forgotten. They will buy the house.

Solution B (Risky)

Subject L hesitates for a moment. In that tiny hesitation, he discovers his own soul. Perhaps there is such a thing as karma. Perhaps his past evil actions are the direct cause of this stench. He cannot force this innocent couple to smell his fart *and* buy this horrible little house. But there's no way he's going to come clean. None of them want that.

Subject L (halfway down the stairs): Oh my god!

As they crowd out of the tiny coffin room, **Gary** and **Jane** freeze.

Subject L: That's gross – can you smell that?

The sorely unpleasant smell is everywhere. **Gary** and **Jane** nod dumbly.

Subject L: Okay, I'll come clean. This house, it's haunted. There was a double murder here in the 90s and the bodies were hidden under the floorboards, right there on the landing.

It is patently impossible for this to be the case, unless they were the bodies of rodents. But they let him continue.

Subject L: And the smell – that's how the killer was caught . . .

Gary: But it smells like an egg and cheeseburger.

Subject L: That's *exactly* what the victim had for breakfast . . . that's how they pinned it on him . . . CCTV . . .

Jane (shuddering): Ooh. Horrible!

Subject L: Let's get out of here. I'm totally psyched that we actually got to smell the phantom stench. The

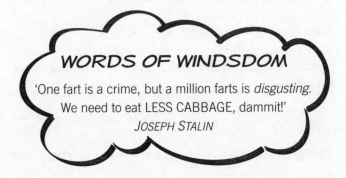

WORDS OF WINDSDOM

'One fart is a crime, but a million farts is *disgusting*.
We need to eat LESS CABBAGE, dammit!'
JOSEPH STALIN

guys in the office will go mental. You guys are so lucky. Now, you're going to *love* the next place . . .

Solution C (Kamikaze)

As **Subject L** stands still, he watches the poor quiet couple stumble into the fart cloud and then freeze as they suddenly become aware of something very unpleasant.

Subject L (grinning hungrily): Any problems?

Gary: I guess – not. So far, I guess . . .

Subject L giggles, gives them a thumbs-up and sprints out of the house.

When they follow him outside, **Subject L** has already placed himself on the other side of the fence in next door's garden. He starts talking at the top of his voice.

Subject L: He didn't have a chance! Listen, darling, after the trick he played on me nearly cost me my job there was no messing around. So I went round to his place last night and dosed him up with sleeping tablets. Then I picked up his clients, pretending to be him, brought them to this house . . . and *farted in front of them*! Come on, bro, this is the benefit of being an identical twin. You get to pull off such a sweet revenge . . .

Then, before **Gary** and **Jane** can find their way round the fence and confront him, **Subject L** has scampered down the side of the house and into the overgrown back garden. He jumps a wire fence and scrambles out into what seems to be derelict wasteland. The sky darkens. In his peripheral vision he catches sight of a homeless man moving towards him.

Subject L's body is found four days later.

WORDS OF WINDSDOM

'Around the Cape we came across a land of giant savages –
men who wore their stomachs on their heads and belched
out cloudy gusts of sweet perfume. It was about then
we worked out to STOP EATING the local mushrooms.'
FERDINAND MAGELLAN

FARTS THAT CHANGED HISTORY

'Softly, softly, secret farty.'
Schoolboy proverb

The only person who is known to have communicated by farting alone is Jimmy 'The Weirdo' McGee, who was sent to solitary confinement in Alcatraz prison in 1939 for the murder of his three wives. He was never released, but the man in the next cell, Massimiliano 'the Half-breed' Llewellyn, claimed that Jimmy (his guts ravaged by wartime prison food) communicated with him nightly by farting in Morse code. Llewellyn would respond by tapping on his false leg. At first they just chatted, then

FARTING WORLD RECORDS

LOUDEST RECORDED FART
Recorded in Scarborough in 1901, where Tommy 'Bruce Baggy Bag Bag' McSteen, a local entertainer, could be seen on stage each night at the Lazy Flamingo using his colonic bursts as replacement for the bass drum. Its exact decibel level was not noted, but it is the only fart in history known to have pierced an eardrum – Tommy's own, after complaints led the council to forcibly apply a butt-plug that caused his system to backfire.

played games of chess. Finally, McGee dictated his entire autobiography to Llewellyn, who memorized the whole thing and later had it published under the title *Life's a Gas*. The title proved bitterly ironic for Llewellyn, who was ultimately indicted for the murder of a New Jersey pawnshop owner and sent to the gas chamber.

'Beware the farting sparrow; he is a total dickhead.'
Old cockney proverb

One of the big reveals in President Franklin D. Roosevelt's published diaries was that he had nicknames for all his different farts. Names included the 'surprised duck', the 'pneumatic drill', the 'accelerating motorbike', the 'colonel's harrumph', the 'squeaky hinge', the 'pop', the 'cheerful hello', the 'tiny tickler', the 'whining dog', the 'tiger's roar' and the 'foghorn'. His diary entry for 14 December 1941 reads: 'Difficult meeting with Stalin today. Rum fellow. We agreed terms at last but then I surprised him with a squeaky hinge following hard upon a whining dog, and he wasn't happy. The fate of the world hung in the balance.'

WORDS OF WINDSDOM

'Nonviolence is the weapon of the strong. That said, if you fart like that again I will smash your teeth down your throat.'
MAHATMA GANDHI

Although a stabilizing influence in British politics, Caroline of Ansbach, consort to George II, had less of a firm control upon her own insides, as she proved when she became one of the few people in history thought to have been killed by a fart. Aged fifty-four, the German princess became agonisingly constipated and, after many days of doctors failing to ease her pain, her stomach exploded. As she was dying, she was taken on a stretcher through London. Some witnesses said that as she passed diners sitting outside a restaurant, she pointed to her wounds and advised them, 'Don't order the sausages.'

'History is like an egg salad. If you don't pay close attention, it will repeat on you.'
Proverb

While competing at the 1976 Montreal Olympics, Belgian athlete Sylvain Grescholt attempted to boost himself to gold in the triple jump with a blended concoction containing forty Scotch bonnet peppers. The plan backfired, as did his intestines, and the result looked like one of splatter-horror maestro Dario Argento's gorier efforts. The athletics were suspended for the afternoon while organizers facilitated a complete change of sand and Grescholt became the recipient of the world's first prosthetic colon.

FARTING WORLD RECORDS

MOST PATRIOTIC FART

In occupied Italy during the Second World War, the Nazis kept a popular radio soap opera on the air to help boost public morale. The country's favourite character was a comical bumbling priest, who often broke wind with great gusto. The actor was, however, a member of the Resistance, and his farts were in fact carefully timed signals to his compadres, warning of German manoeuvres. It is said that the actor's obedient sphincter saved the lives of hundreds of brave Italians.

WORDS OF WINDSDOM

'We shall fart in France. We shall fart on the seas, we shall fart with growing confidence and growing strength . . . We shall never surrender our Blenkinsop's tinned curried kidneys, 3d from all good retailers!'

ADVERT WRITTEN BY WINSTON CHURCHILL DURING HIS EARLY DAYS IN THE FOOD INDUSTRY

The slowest fart ever recorded was by centenarian Mabel 'DJ Savage Beats' Hamworthy. It began on the eve of her 102nd birthday and continued for four days, until a carer switched on her bedside light, igniting over 300 pints of escaped gas. Three were killed and fourteen injured in the explosion.

'Is the dog chasing his own tail? Or is he just angry with his butthole?'
Native American proverb

The stupidest bottom burp has often been attributed to someone called Rick in Britain but in fact it was performed by Henry Carter. A famously intrepid tightrope artist, in 1932 Carter crossed Niagara Falls on a length of fishing wire while riding a unicycle in order to win the hand of his circus sweetheart, the forty-five-stone Juliet, the 'Beast of Croyden'. He was carrying a microphone, intending to propose to her in front of the crowd when he reached halfway. But nerves got the better of him and he farted instead, falling to his death before 10,000 mildly amused onlookers.

FARTING WORLD RECORDS

EARLIEST DETECTABLE FART

In 1927, when Egyptologists uncovered the tomb of Thutmosis VI in Luxor, they found an apparently empty receptacle alongside the one containing the pharaoh's kidneys and lungs. When opened, however, the stench that emanated from it was profoundly disturbing and is widely supposed to be the final sacred fart of the dead pharaoh. Indeed, the Curse of the Mummy's Fart was notorious for a while, as the three men who smelt it all died soon after in unrelated gas leakages. It was thought that, after farting, the only way to 'lift the curse' was to 'walk like an Egyptian' for ten minutes.

The bestselling farting fictional character in the world is FartyPants McBottomBurp, a popular cartoon character who appears on greetings cards (and other merchandise) in Finland. Although his name is jaunty, the character displays the nation's famously morbid temperament, and bestselling cards in the series include 'Happy 10th birthday – we're all going to die one day' and 'Ashes to ashes, dust to dust, happy christening, there isn't a god'.

One of the earliest professional sports in Scotland was golf. However, it was not a desire for bracing outdoor sports that led to the creation of the game, but the reluctance of Scottish wives to allow their husbands back into the family home after a lunchtime of whisky, beer and offal boiled in sheep's stomach. Once the excluded men had turned their daily exile into something that could be gambled on, rules were needed, and the game was born.

WORDS OF WINDSDOM

'It is better by noble boldness to run the risk of being subject to half the evils we anticipate than to remain in cowardly listlessness for fear of what might happen.

Yes, that's my excuse and I'm sticking to it.

Live your own fucking life.'

HERODOTUS

CHOOSE YOUR OWN FARTVENTURE

You are presented with a variety of
embarrassing scenarios you may have
encountered in real life. But this time
you get to choose how you act and see
how it plays out – this will determine
whether you successfully negotiate the
dangers of being a prolific farter and
come out smelling of roses, or whether
you suffer a dire social death.

1: THE FIRST DATE

1. The night before the date. Your housemate is keen to go out for a pint. Knowing him, it could easily get out of hand. But you could really do with one to quieten your nerves and help you sleep. Do you a) go for a drink with him or b) not?

A) Go to number 2
B) Go to number 6

2. In the pub with your housemate, you want something gentle on the stomach but he buys you a strong ale with a whisky chaser and chilli peanuts, which look oh-so-tempting after your sensible salad dinner. Do you a) accept or do you b) stick to your plan of having one drink (giving him your whisky), a bit of a chinwag and going home?

A) Go to number 10
B) Go to number 3

3. After work the next day you freshen up in the work loos and get to the pub fifteen minutes early. The weather is clement and you sit at a table outside. With the third sip of your drink you light a cigarette – your first of the day. Two puffs in and you experience a plummeting feeling in your gut followed by an acute desire to fart. The sharpness of the sensation suggests it will be a nasty, intense one. There's nobody at the tables immediately surrounding you. Do you a) let it fly and enjoy the moment of risk or b) struggle to hold the evil in?

A) Go to number 4
B) Go to number 6

4. No sooner have you detected the revolting smell than there your date is, just a few metres away. It's impossible – until a moment ago the street was gloriously empty. And now there they are, smiling and waving, wandering towards you like some tragic innocent into a dangerous warzone of smell.

You have to make a swift calculation. You can't be sure, but the dreadful odour seems to be dissipating. Do you a) smile, wave your date over and trust your luck, or b) leap up, rush to greet them and guide them indoors while uttering inanities?

A) Go to number 5
B) Go to number 6

5. No sooner does your date sit down than they become clearly uncomfortable. Your confidence was unwarranted: you've been caught out as a stinky farter. You go inside and order dinner, and your date follows with unhappy reluctance. As you're scanning the menu your date makes a

dramatic excuse about an ill relative and leaves. You go back to your table outside and sit alone, thinking about what you've done.

6. You find a table in the restaurant section of the pub and your date begins. Your date is called Sam. If you're dating a man, he is a confident, engaging sort of chap who doesn't seem to realize how handsome he is. If Sam is a woman, then she is good looking, funny and relaxed.

You are totally out of your league. It dawns on you that your 'healthy lunch' of lentil salad wasn't the sensible option after all – it was a time bomb. You are dying to fart so hard you can barely think. But you've only just sat down and Sam's drink hasn't yet arrived. Do you a) make a brief excuse and slip off to the toilet, or b) stick it out for another ten minutes, just so you don't look like an early-toilet-going freak?

A) Go to number 7
B) Go to number 8

7. Once the cubicle door is closed you let out your big resounding fart and then for safety's sake sit on the toilet for two or three minutes, sitting up straight and then bending over to try and squeeze out any other subversive elements. As you stand up to leave, another big one rips through you.

Good to have that out with, you think.

When you return to the table, Sam has ordered two of the tapas dishes you most adore in the whole world. But they are both certain to scorch through what is an already tempestuous colon. Do you a) pretend to eat a few mouthfuls of each before creating a diversion and spitting them into your napkin, or b) enjoy the taste of them and swallow, then wait for the terrifying results?

A) Go to number 9
B) Go to number 8

8. Before long you are struggling to put a sentence together owing to your intense intestinal discomfort, and you fail to notice a young child on a nearby table fiddling with a balloon near to a naked flame. It presently bursts.

The sound makes you fart uncontrollably. And not, alas, an instant blast in unison with the popping balloon: it's a long rasp that tapers towards an upward inflection. It leaves a question mark hanging in the air between you and Sam. You're toast. Sam fakes an urgent telephone call and leaves.

9. You successfully distract Sam's attention for a few seconds by making him or her turn round, then spit out your mouthful and scrape the food from your plate onto the napkin in your lap.

Sam turns back round. You now have a small mound of food on the napkin in your lap and notice an unleashed dog from another table ambling towards you. You wave the dog away. But it noses beneath the table, seeking out your crotch.

Do you a) give it a subtle but sharp slap round the head to send it on its way and risk being caught looking like a dreadful animal hater, or b) with a skilful flick of the wrist, attempt to toss the filled napkin under the empty table behind you?

A) Go to number 12

B) Go to number 13

10. Arriving home later in a victorious mood, you go to the bathroom and come back into the kitchen to find that your housemate has poured two glasses of red wine. Good man! You have been farting pretty much constantly for the last three hours.

You had ale, whisky, cider and (as a forfeit after losing a game of pool) tequila. But now wine is in front of you, you know you'll consume it. Just like the garlicky, chilli-saucey lamb doner that your housemate has slopped onto a plate between you.

Your chances of making it in for work later are slim, and as for being in any condition for your date, you fear the worst. Do you a) try to postpone the date or b) go through with it?

A) Go to number 11
B) Go to number 6

11. Your date does not reply. That's it, buster. Last chance you'll have with someone that good looking. Just for one stupid little extra drink with your dickhead housemate. Well done. It's over.

12. You would HIT a DOG? To cover your own FART? Fair enough. You smack the animal on the side of the skull. It growls and snaps at your hand. You yelp in surprise. The dog locks teeth with your napkin. You pull. The dog pulls harder.

'Get off me you little . . .' you begin. You stand up.

At last the napkin tears and the contents flop wetly onto the floor.

You are left panting. You catch sight of Sam,

whose eyes are now narrowed in shrewd evaluation. You know that look – the look of someone mentally recording an event to be repeated often as a treasured anecdote.

The dog is happily licking the pat of mush from the floor.

You open your mouth in surprise as you feel a very, very large fart thunder through your nether regions, in the key of G sharp.

I think this date is over.

13. Sam detects nothing as you ball the serviette and fling it beneath the table behind. As an adversary, the dog is instantly bested.

After this, the evening starts going smoothly. You are enjoying yourself and order some digestively placid dish, distracting Sam with one of your funniest anecdotes

Then you smell something. Something unpleasant. You look up and Sam is smiling conspiratorially at you. You begin to wonder whether this smell belongs to Sam. It's undeniably farty. And who else could it be? You wonder whether Sam is inviting you to join a secret group of people who are not afraid of their own smells. It makes you feel uncomfortable, but Sam's charming smile invites confidence.

Do you a) let the one you've been storing up quietly leak out, to show Sam that you are game, or b) make an excuse and go to the bathroom again, to allow the awkward moment to pass?

A) Go to number 14
B) Go to number 15

14. You are both leaning in now, chatting across the table conspiratorially. You've instinctively forged an easy intimacy. Except as you inch closer to each other you see Sam's nose wrinkle. Your date regards you sceptically.

'I . . . I hate to ask this,' Sam says, 'but did you just fart?'

For some reason this is the last question you expected. What was the smell then . . . ? You turn your head and see the dog still chewing away under the table behind you, his backside pointed at your head. Oh.

In response you succeed only in shaking your head and uttering weak denials. Sam would never understand your reason for openly breaking wind in the middle of a date, just as you can't comprehend why Sam was impervious to the dog's fart until just now. But that's life.

Sam folds the napkin, leaves money for the food ordered and politely excuses themself.

15. You scurry off down the spiral staircase, aware this is your second toilet break already and the mains haven't even arrived yet. So it must be your last for a while and you must make the best of it. This is when you find that since your last visit the toilets have inexplicably become out of order. You let off a massive smelly grunt in protest.

But this makes you want to fart a whole lot more.

Should you a) cut your losses and return to the table, pretending to have gone, and trust your luck, or b) decide your physical need is too great, and run over the road to the Irish pub and go to the toilet there?

A) Go to number 16
B) Go to number 17

16. You make a show of ambling back to the table across the restaurant in order to hide your excruciating discomfort. But when you sit down, Sam (wonderful Sam!) simply says, 'My turn!' and disappears off to the bathroom.

Sweet deliverance. Once Sam is out of sight you let out a victory blast. There's plenty more where that came from – in fact, you're so amply supplied you think you could parp out the first movement of Mozart's Horn Concerto No.4.

Sam returns and shortly afterwards your food arrives. The evening proceeds well. You pay your bill, then enjoy a pleasant walk together towards the Tube station. You are surprised to learn that Sam lives nearby – and all of a sudden you are both talking enthusiastically about one last drink at Sam's place.

Do you a) decide that this is pushing your luck too far, claim an early meeting and head for the station, knowing you will see Sam again soon, or b) decide damn it, why not enjoy yourself? That trouble earlier in the evening is behind you. Sam is too good to resist.

A) Go to number 18
B) Go to number 19

17. It's fine – you'll only take a second. But you can't go back through the pub – Sam will see you. The only other door nearby is the kitchen. You walk through quickly, head down, dash out the back door, cross the road and dive into the pub.

At the bottom of the stairs you discover that these toilets are out of order too! Not just out of order – there's *police tape* over the entrance. Through gritted teeth you rage at fate's insolence.

You're about to leave when a man backs into you. He is one of a team of three carrying a new ice machine down to the cellar. There's no way past!

But you refuse to give up. You open a door marked STAFF ONLY and trot diffidently through a dark, smear-tiled kitchen. You race up the two flights of stairs and, turning a corner, go through a door to find yourself in someone's front room. A toothless old man glances vacantly at you from beside the television.

You sprint out and through the front door before he has a chance to say anything. The door slams shut.

Where the hell are you now? The pub isn't even visible from here. Not just the one you're heading back to – the one you've just left. How is that possible?

You're in a cobbled alleyway. There's traffic drifting past at each end. A) right or b) left?

A) Go to number 20
B) Go to number 21

18. Well done. You did it. Successfully navigated a total obstacle course of a date with one of the most severe and distracting of handicaps. If you can do it once, you can do it again. And again. For you and Sam are to be married, and to spend quite a few years together until . . . well, let's not go into that right now. You're in a good mood and on the way to the Tube let out a series of high-octane stinkers in celebration, one with each step. Parp. Parp. Parpity parp.

19. God, you're a real sucker for punishment, aren't you? Just don't know when to give up. No sooner are you in Sam's flat than you are visited by those familiar gremlins who tunnel through your insides, battling to get out. It's worse than ever.

Sam goes to fetch a drink from the kitchen and you think you can get away with a small one, just to ease the tension. But you're wrong, baby – you just opened the fartgates! In attempting to let out a tiny squeaker you give voice to a colossal juggernaut that sounds like a controlled explosion in a neighbouring field. It lifts you clean off the sofa and suffuses the room with an unmistakeable farmyard stench. You lock eyes with Sam standing in the doorway, holding two drinks.

You don't even say 'I'll get my coat'. You just get your coat.

20. You sprint to the end of the alley and into the street, out of sight. This isn't right either. Oh shit. You're stepping between the stalls of a marketplace packing up for the evening. How long have you been gone now? Ten minutes? Suddenly across the street a number 18 bus pulls up. The 18 stops right next to the pub you were in! You get on and sit down, feeling once more this date could still go well. It's only when the bus crosses the river that you realize you have been travelling the wrong way. You are now about two miles from the pub.

You begin mentally to compose a very compli-cated apology to Sam. You will have to make up some sort of logical reason for why you've skipped out on the date, because the truth will most certainly not do.

21. You clatter out of the end of the alleyway to find yourself opposite the pub and spot Sam sitting there in the window. Your date blinks, then smiles quizzically, head cocked to one side. By the time you reach the pub door you are freed of unwanted gas and have decided to come clean with Sam. You leave out the stuff about needing to fart, of course, but make it a story of an innocent person's desperate dash for the loo. Your honesty pays dividends: Sam thinks this is possibly the funniest thing they have ever heard. They can't stop laughing about it throughout the meal, and in a good way.

You both have a great time and leave at the end of the night (after a brief canoodle by the railway station entrance) exuding happiness. You've already arranged to see each other next week. And you're sure something good will come of this.

SCENARIOS
7–10

(INTERMEDIATE)

SURVIVAL SCENARIO 7:
IN THE PANTOMIME HORSE

Subject C is a happily married mother of two. A 'quiet, unassuming woman' is how most people think of her. But when the chance to be in the village pantomime came along she surprised herself by being desperate to be in it.

Subject C was a little insulted by the role she was given, especially once it became apparent that they were giving a speaking role to everyone else, even Bernard Trubshaw, who drools so appallingly since his stroke. But now she's determined to be the best damn pantomime horse ever. The other cast were clearly startled at the dress rehearsal to catch sight of her 'pimped up' horse costume, to which she had added eyelashes, lipstick, a gaudy nose stud and some provocative prison 'tats. (The director's objections eventually died away when **Subject C** asked why 'a fictional horse *couldn't* have a bloody tattoo?')

Finally the first night is here. In retrospect **Subject C** is pleased she didn't get the second female lead, the role she had her eye on – she didn't realize the part required as much brassy sexual innuendo as that. And frankly old Mrs Stipplewell from the antiques shop is bringing it off with more élan than anyone could have expected.

Subject C is certainly not underplaying her own part either – she goes everywhere with a maximum amount of stamping and neighing and tossing of head. So far this is an absolute winner with the audience. The only person who has a problem with it is **Randolph**, **Subject C**'s American neighbour, who's playing the back end of the horse. He's really not enjoying it and keeps whispering viciously every time she bucks and kicks.

This is her big chance to shine so he can just lump it, **Subject C** thinks. That is, until she farts. They're on stage. Mid-scene. It just slips out. One of those thin little ones that burns your bum-lips as it escapes. Pure concentrated evil.

WHAT DOES SUBJECT C DO?

Solution A (Sane)

Subject C only has about one second before **Randolph** smells it. And after that about three seconds max before he freaks out in a very public way. **Subject C**'s kids are here too – everyone's night will be ruined!

The action in the play requires no movement on the part of the horse in this section. Therefore **Subject C** feels safe as she reaches around behind her and grabs the top of **Randolph**'s skull with one hand, then places her fingers over his nostrils with the other.

Subject C (whispering): It's for the best, Randolph!

He begins to wriggle, but the rear-end of the horse costume doesn't leave much room for arm movement. He opens his mouth to gasp for breath but the sound is lost among the overacting by the rest of the cast. However, **Randolph** doesn't make the fuss she expected. **Subject C** assumes that (as a brainiac theoretician by trade) he has made some sort of conceptual leap from her actions to the possible cause for her actions, and may in fact be grateful she has prevented him from involuntarily smelling her flatus. Either way, he has ceased to struggle.

Subject C waits until the smell has passed before letting go of his nostrils. As they exit, stage left, they both make a mental note not to sign up for next year's panto.

Solution B (Risky)

There's nothing to be done. **Randolph**'s smelling it already.

Subject C has broken one of the profound laws of society by farting in someone's face. So to hell with her characterization. For **Randolph**'s sake (and not because of her newly discovered lust for attention), and before he has had a chance to react, she rears up.

'Neigh!' she shouts at the top of her voice (rather than actually neighing), before careering forward across the stage. **Randolph,** trapped inside the suit, his senses thrown into violent confusion by the horrific smell, is powerless to do anything but follow her. The cider-addled crowd seem to imagine that this is a planned part of the proceedings and mass hysteria erupts in the room. She showboats as outrageously as she can for a few more seconds, neighing like it's going out of bloody fashion. Then she careens off down the side of the hall, through the fire exit and into the car park, where she stands, exalting for a moment, watching her horsey breath evaporate into the night air. Showbiz! Greasepaint! Isn't it *magic*?

Subject C hears a groan from behind her as **Randolph** starts to recover.

Solution C (Kamikaze)

Frankly, **Subject C** has never liked **Randolph**. She has an even longer acquaintance, however, with her own acidy farts, and she wouldn't wish those on anyone. It's just not on – the gig is up. She unbuttons the costume, then steps out (followed by a cloud of slightly diffused bum gas) and stands on the stage, blinking. The male and female leads are slightly fazed, and stop speaking. A stunned silence descends on the hall.

Subject C: Sorry, I farted. (She gestures at **Randolph**, who is blinking bemusedly through his spectacles.) It was a bit stinky for him, so we had to lose the costume. Carry on, everyone.

From the audience **Subject C** can recognize her own husband's laughter, a sound she finds deeply comforting. **Randolph**, stunned to find himself exposed like this, nods and then resumes his position bent forward, his head at her backside. The pantomime proceeds, with **Subject C** and **Randolph** performing a somewhat Brechtian interpretation of a horse in full view of everyone, and to the continuing amusement of everyone, especially **Subject C**'s husband, who along with their kids and many others give them a standing ovation at the end.

Subject C's family may remember the fart. But most of all what they will remember is being proud of their mum and wife like never before.

SURVIVAL SCENARIO 8:
THE CROWDED LIFT

It's lunch. The lift is pretty full when **Subject K** gets into it. He doesn't like crowded lifts. He doesn't like people, or work, or the world. Everyone's squeezed in next to each other. **Subject K** shouldn't have got in the lift so close to lunchtime. He's already regretting everything: going to lunch before 1 p.m., taking this job, continuing to breathe.

Whenever he's in a crowded lift like this, **Subject K** has an insane impulse to do stupid, nonsensical things. Today he's got this ridiculous desire to flap his wings and quack like a duck. He gets a chest-tightening enjoyment in the anticipation of the feeling of fear he would inspire in the others. They'd really freak out. The stupid boring sheep. Stuck in their *pens*. When he'd finished quacking he'd stare at them and scream 'I'M NOT MAD!'

When two more people squeeze into the crush at the next floor, cramming **Subject K** against some poor helpless tiny bloke, he's so outraged that he forgets he was trying desperately to control a violent fart. His bowels, given their slip of a chance, ring lustily forth. The lift doors close with a ping. It's a *smelly* one.

WHAT DOES SUBJECT K DO?

Solution A (Sane)

Coward's way out. Can't beat it.

'Shit!' **Subject K** shouts, as though he's just remembered something. 'Don't let it close!'

Subject K is not a small man. Twenty years of evenings eating crisps and playing dungeons and dragons and (latterly) *World of Warcraft* have left him with the heft of a small family car. But weight is useful in some scenarios. Some startled stranger's finger dances onto the right button just in time and the door trundles smoothly back open.

At which moment **Subject K** mercilessly flexes his mighty girth, and there is a great groan in the lift. For one moment the humans inside it are individuals no longer: they are part of a swelling human tide, breaking against the walls. They moan in concerted misery as they are crushed against each other, chest to chest, face to back, shoulder to groin. An instant later **Subject K** is free of the crush, which is subsiding back to fill the space behind him with a collective gasp of outraged probity.

He hops it – disappears through the nearest door as the lift closes once more with a ping. A ping pong, in fact. **Subject K** doesn't look back. He's pretty sure it all happened too fast for them to get a decent look at him (although his size will obviously narrow the list of suspects). Now they're stuck in the elevator with the odour. Tough shit. Life's not fair.

Maybe he'll take the stairs. He's been meaning to do that for years. Twelve stories. Burn a few calories before lunch. Things are looking up! He searches around him for a light switch as the door clicks shut behind him. With the last shaft of disappearing light, **Subject K** discovers he is locked in the cleaning cupboard.

Solution B (Risky)

Oh dear. Fart smell spreading. No way to escape – for **Subject K** or any of them. All of a sudden, eyes still shut fast, he starts singing.

Subject K: *Kum-ba-ya, my lord, kum-ba-ya . . .*

At once, everyone in the lift feels the same sinking feeling. The opening line of that hymn takes them all back to assembly in school, wearing uncomfortable uniforms, sitting on a cold floor. Afraid of that proportion of classmates who already hate them, or who will inevitably soon start to hate them.

Subject K: *Someone's crying lord, kum-ba-ya . . .*

Everyone in the lift is lost in their own miserable childhood flashbacks (as well as bitterly resenting whoever the fruitcake is who's singing that hymn in a crowded lift – what is this, Speaker's Corner?). As the doors open, they all disperse into the building's lobby, weighed down by sad thoughts about a multitude of things, but no longer wondering about that smell which was, if anything, a welcome distraction from their forlorn recollections.

Solution C (Kamikaze)

A moment's startled panic and **Subject K** comes up with a brilliant solution. Everyone is packed like sardines into this thing, no one can move so much as a shoulder to look round, or see who's talking to who.

Subject K (adopting the rough and addled voice of an older sort of gent): What the hell's that smell? Is that from your *arse*, Gerry?

With this utterance he directly addresses the elephant in the lift. Almost everyone is already thinking something along these lines. What's more, the doors are closing and everyone is facing a grim twenty seconds in this warm enveloping fug.

For his second character he assumes a voice lighter and

more gentle than his own – the voice he gave (when playing with his Star Wars figures) to the begging victim, who was about to be annihilated. Light, fluttery, eager to please.

Subject K (younger voice): No, no – look here, Toby.

Subject K (older voice): What's in that? Christ, that stinks!

Subject K (younger voice): *Sssh*, Toby. It's cheese! You know Mina's addicted to the stuff. You should have smelt our car on the way home from France at the weekend. It does pong a bit, doesn't it?

Subject K (older voice): Like a pig's arse.

God, I'm so sharp, thinks **Subject K**, I could cut myself.

He can detect the relaxation throughout the lift, and feels momentarily responsible that the assembled strangers are now breathing in his revolting fumes with relish, imagining themselves at a French picnic.

As the lift approaches the ground floor, **Subject K** feels suddenly sad to be about to lose his new creations. He feels there's more mileage in them.

Subject K (older voice): So did the weekend away do the trick, my boy? Has she overlooked your little indiscretion?

Subject K (younger voice, whispering urgently): Toby!

Subject K (older voice): And did the antibiotics work, by the way?

Subject K (younger voice): *Ssssh*, Toby!

The lift goes ping. No one is thinking of the fart.

WORDS OF WINDSDOM

HAMLET: There are more things in heaven and earth, Horatio, than are dreamt of in your philosophy.
HORATIO (Farts, then wafts it towards Hamlet): That's what I think of you. Do me a favour and shit off?
HAMLET, ACT I, SCENE V, 167-9 [ORIGINAL FOLIO, DISPUTED BY SOME SCHOLARS]

SURVIVAL SCENARIO 9: WHILE PERFORMING A STRIPTEASE

Stripping is only a side-line for **Subject V**. He mostly works at the car workshop, Len's Autoparts, but Len doesn't always have a shift for him. And if he wants to save up for the wedding he's got to take all the work he can get. Shelly doesn't mind too much that he does this, bless her.

Today it's the upstairs room of a wine bar. **Subject V** changes in the loos and then approaches the table where the hen party are hunched and screaming, wine stains around their mouths. When (after the same corny old intro about needing to perform a police inspection) he starts pulling off his shirt, they go predictably mental.

Subject V prides himself on being able to spot when he has been booked vindictively and the hen is genuinely mortified to the point of unhappiness. So it is today, and therefore after waggling around a bit with the poor undeserving wife-to-be he concentrates on the aunt who booked him, a sharp-faced old crone. But to his consternation, the aunt is into it. Big time. Before he knows it he's on all fours on the table, on top of her, and she's yelping like a harpooned seal.

It's difficult to look at your watch when you're wearing just a thong and some whipped cream, and simulating

rampant sex on a table covered in leftover fajitas. When **Subject V** finally catches sight of the clock and sees he's still got another full fifteen minutes left, the thought loosens his bowels. A great big, smelly guff escapes.

WHAT DOES SUBJECT V DO?

Solution A (Sane)

It would be bad enough already, but now three of the women are filming **Subject V** with their phones. Where does this end? Will they film him dancing while they contort their faces in disgust? Then post the videos on Facebook? Will he be an internet sensation before he's got the smell of salsa and guacamole out of his chest hair?

He abruptly stands up. The women misunderstand and scream some more. The fifty-something aunt stretched out between his legs is writhing and twisting around so much she looks like she'll put her back out.

Subject V gets down from the table and taking an unused napkin removes the whipped cream (and sour cream, jalapenos, grated cheddar) from his torso. He pulls on his trousers and places his faux-police tabard around his shoulders. Then, impervious to the pleading, which turns into accusatory screams, he walks downstairs and over the road to the cashpoint. He withdraws a full refund and takes it back to the aunt, whose fury has abated, and who is cackling again, glass of wine in hand. She doesn't thank him or really acknowledge his repayment. In the drunken hysteria, no one seems to have noticed the odious smell.

On the way home **Subject V** is unrepentant. Wedding or no wedding, Shelly can't expect him to put up with this. He is twenty-four. He is too old for this shit.

Solution B (Risky)

Subject V realizes that the ladies are looking at him aghast. He shouldn't have had curry leftovers for lunch. Especially not with extra pepper sauce on it. Not before a booking!

He can see from their faces he's in danger of not getting paid at all. Shelly will have his balls. He has to win them back. Shelly, and his balls.

Someone's bought the hen a bottle of Sambuca, perhaps for later. Spotting a lighter on the table, **Subject V** grabs the bottle, twists off the top and pours it over his chest. He flips the lighter and his chest ignites. It hurts more than he could ever have imagined.

He jumps. He screams. He runs round in circles. He rushes out the door and into the road, narrowly missing a bread truck that screeches to a halt. **Subject V** dashes over to the nearby canal and jumps in. The water is disgusting but the relief of it is like nothing he's ever felt before. As he looks up at the wine bar across the road he sees a gaggle of women leaning out of the window, cheering his performance. In fact, they love it so much they're dropping fivers into the street – tips!

At this moment **Subject V** can't help thinking: I really should have stayed in school.

Solution C (Kamikaze)

Unless he's sadly mistaken, it seems to **Subject V** that far from considering that he has just broken some social code, his audience actually seem to *like* it. It's like his musk, or something. It seems to make them hungrier.

They're chanting now, clapping and chanting as he prowls up and down the table, roaring like a lion. Usually it's a lot extra for the full monty, but what the hell – he whips off the thong. At last he's poised, back arched, groin to the ceiling, when he feels the rogan josh twinge. The depraved women are still chanting. They want something more of **Subject V**: further, darker, more twisted. So he goes with it, and two sharp bursts of ex-curry land on the table behind him.

Subject V twists his head, looking round at them in sudden shame.

They are still. Someone kills the music. Fourteen minutes later there is a blanket round **Subject V**'s shoulder and he's being taken into custody under section 28 of the Mental Health Act, where he will remain under observation for three weeks. Still, no one remembers the original fart. So: mission accomplished.

WORDS OF WINDSDOM

'To every action there is an equal and opposite reaction. For instance, Mrs Scuddingthorpe's delicious oyster and kidney pie that I had for lunch and the monstrous guff I just wafted in your direction.'
ISAAC NEWTON

SURVIVAL SCENARIO 10: WHILE PILOTING THE DEATH STAR

I bet you think that piloting the *Death Star* is easy, don't you? Well it *bloody isn't*. Just ask **Subject O**. He's been doing it for just over a year and it's a *living nightmare*. Most people assume there's just three buttons: Go, Stop and Destroy Planet. Well, there are in fact over 24,000 buttons. And you can't get any sleep with the alarms going off all the time.

And Death Stars just *don't work*. Everything's broken! The executive toilets have been backed up all week. And the entire ship's lights flicker once every ten seconds, which freaks everyone out. Plus, why doesn't anyone in Engineering speak the same language as each other?

Today is a big day. Everyone on the bridge is in full dress uniform, standing at attention in two straight lines ready to perform an all-systems run-through. Stupid uniform: chafes your neck like buggery and is no friend to the officer with oversized testicles (not that he's going to share that with anyone). Who designed this thing?

But no time for that, the moment of truth has arrived. **Subject O** stands in front of the crew and gives the order to start engines.

Nothing happens.

Except, a second later, **Subject O** farts. No sound in space, my arse, he thinks. Or no sound *except* my arse. It's a big old toot on the botty trumpet.

WHAT DOES SUBJECT O DO?

Solution A (Sane)

The fart was *perfectly* timed, a ringing little comic parp. Everyone heard it. It's an instant all-time number one piece of admiralty gossip. **Subject O** realizes he's got less than two seconds to react in a way either befitting a respectable captain (impossible) or, instead, befitting someone who has every intention of getting away with a loud fart.

The next moment the engines fire up. Everyone is still staring at him. He decides to adopt an uncharacteristically raffish and friendly tone.

Subject O: Woah, what a relief, eh? Was worried there for a moment. I mean, I totally thought that thing wasn't going to work.

They continue to stare at him.

Subject O: Because that would be, like, a bummer. We don't want a visit from that Darth Vader guy, do we? I mean – what a turbo creep. Am I right?

This little pep talk doesn't seem to be having the desired effect. He was hoping to inspire a slightly school's-out atmosphere, to encourage people to let their hair down a little. But they are all standing as rigidly as ever. Thinking about his fart, no doubt.

Subject O: He's like (adopts an imitation of **Darth Vader**'s breathy rattle) 'I'm Darth Vader, I'm so great'. Yeah? I got the voice didn't I? 'I'm Darth Vader, blah blah blah. I'm so important.'

Still nothing. They just stare.

Subject O: He's standing behind me, isn't he?

Nobody moves, but in response he feels a sudden constriction in his throat. No mention will ever be made of the fart.

Solution B (Risky)

The moment after **Subject O** breaks wind, of course, the lights come back on. Everyone maintains their rigid stance. There is only one thought consuming everyone in the room right now, he knows, and that is his unholy fart. Must distract them somehow.

Subject O (in the stiffly ingratiating tones of a trendy vicar): You know what? *Death Star.* Isn't that just a bit gloomy? Don't you think?

He pauses, cocking his ear as though genuinely waiting for an answer. When inevitably no one responds, he nods as though the silence is proof of consent.

Subject O: Hmm. I mean, *Death Star.* It's just so . . . I'm not an ogre, after all. Why can't we *like* the place we work? 'Rainbow Rocket' perhaps? Or the . . . what do you think . . . 'Happy Place'. Or both!

The assembled admiralty maintain their rigid pose. **Subject O** is now fully cognisant that he's screwed the pooch in a very big way. The only thing that could save him now is to keep going, and try to get himself sectioned.

Subject O: Yes. (Looks about him.) Nice smell . . . Walk and talk . . . Roof . . . Hand . . . Place . . . that I am. That's it! It will be a refreshing change. (He addresses a young man whose name is Kevin) Susan! Take down this order at once. *Death Star* to change its name to Rainbow Rocket Happy Place Nice Smell Walk and Talk Roof Hand Place That I Am. Well chop, chop, girl!

Then he turns and sees **Darth Vader** striding towards him.

Subject O: Oh fuckity pissflaps, I'm screwed.

But luckily for **Subject O**, Darth Vader has a lot on his mind and dealing with eccentric Death Star commanders is low down on his list of pressing priorities.

In a few moments **Subject O** finds himself relieved of his position and quarantined. Three days later, he is retired from the fleet with full honours and a comfy pension.

Solution C (Kamikaze)

The instant after **Subject O** farts, the engines fire up, the control banks blink on. And then he spots **Darth Vader** out of the corner of his eye. Watching. Taking it all in. Preparing a report for the Emperor, no doubt. What the blithering hell can **Subject O** do? Staring like a particularly stupid and nervous rabbit caught in some extra-massive headlights, he totters over to the controls.

Subject O: Smashing. Well, everything seems to be working well. Good old, er, ship, you know.

He fiddles with the controller. The *Death Star* swerves to the left.

Subject O: Oopsy. (Giggles.)

He nervously over-adjusts it with both hands. The *Death Star* lurches violently. Everyone falls over.

Subject O (as he clambers back to his feet): Me and my, er – oh.

Not great last words, really. But then, even if he came out with a corker, there would be no one to record it. Because he's popped the *Death Star* right in the direction of a massive asteroid, going at top speed. **Darth Vader** is freaking out. Everyone is.

Two seconds later, there's a sizeable bang. And ten seconds after that, they're all dead.

WORDS OF WINDSDOM

'In my travels among the Arabs I came to believe that the printing press was the greatest weapon ever invented. Except, on occasion, for my butthole. Their food goes right through you.'
T. E. LAWRENCE

FARTING WORLD RECORDS

EARLIEST BROADCASTED FART

It's well known that the first words were spoken on the telephone when Alexander Graham Bell telephoned his assistant to say 'Mr Watson – come here! I want to see you.' What's less well known is that Bell was an inveterate prankster, and on receiving the message Watson knew with a heavy heart that the great inventor had summoned him only to smell another of his notoriously vile guffs. The professional relationship soon broke down after Bell took to actually farting down the phone line.

A FARTER'S
ALMANAC OF
WORLD FACTS

✿ The only known statue of someone farting is in Stuttgart-Untertürkheim, in Württemberg, Germany. Made of cast bronze, it shows an elderly man bending over, his face contorted in pain, clutching his backside. Its origins are obscure, but the statue may have been commissioned to celebrate the region's successful trade in turnips, which stretched for a thousand years until the early eighteenth century, and caused an intense intestinal discomfort that led to a widespread pained shuffling among old men known as the 'Stuttgart Hobble'.

'It is an ill wind which blows from a dead gorilla's arse.'
Rwandan proverb

✿ In medieval Siam (now Thailand), monks led lives of such intense contemplation they communicated only with hand signals. After a while, however, the less devout monks discovered an easier way of communicating, by short or long anal outbursts, similar to modern semaphore. A recent resurgence of this technique led to a scandal that resulted in the Thai edition of *Who Wants to be a Millionaire?* being taken off air after a monk walked away with over seventy-five billion baht but several flatulent colleagues were subsequently discovered to have been in the audience clutching encyclopedias.

In his 2008 *New Yorker* article 'Anus Horribilis', Michio Kaku speculated that by the year 2050 people will have learnt to fart in other accents. This will have less effect on, say, the Swiss, who can already fart in French, Italian and Swiss dialects.

In the Arctic, temperatures can be so low that all the moisture from one's breath freezes and falls with a gentle tinkling sound, which is known as the 'ice whisper'. The same is true of farts, the resulting sound known as the 'accusing suggestion'.

> *'The farting pigeon may win the race, but he returns to an empty nest.'*
> **Norwegian proverb**

In the medieval Scottish Highlands it was considered a friendly greeting among warlords for the kilt to be raised and a lusty fart to break forth from their nether regions. Indeed, the 'fart halloo' was something that many chieftains worked hard in their spare time to improve. The mightiest exponent was ninth century laird Ramsay Dunkrieth, also known as the Fartin' Tartan, who once greeted a fellow thane with a gust so profound and powerful that all who witnessed it are said to have burst into tears and vomited at the same time.

❧ Warlords of tribes in Bali have a custom of breaking wind as loudly as possible after a dinner, not only to show appreciation but as a declaration of personal might. However, in the 1970s the leader of the Wutusha tribe found that he was unable to break wind with any violence whatsoever and, having been educated at Eton and Oxford, sought

FARTING WORLD RECORDS

Longest-Range Fart
Although never officially recorded, the longest-range farts in the world are those that carry over many miles of flat Australian desert. Back in the mists of time, Aboriginal tribesmen discovered that the strange acoustics of the arid outback meant that farts could be heard many hundreds of times further away than the human voice. Therefore long-range gusts were used to warn fellow tribe members of attack, or send back blasts of victory after a conflict. It has been speculated that it is owing to this practise that the Aboriginal names for many townships (Toowimba, Ourimbah, Jimbooba, Bullaburra) sound like nicknames for escaping bum-gas.

a technological solution to his problem in the form of a tape recorder. At a crucial tribal conclave after dinner, he unfortunately inserted the wrong cassette and rather than a resounding raspberry, what greeted the diners was 'I'll Be There' by the Jackson Five. The other tribe leaders were stunned, and instantly acknowledged him as a living god.

'Though he does not speak, the man who breaks wind honks like a goose.'
Dutch proverb

In the original and most recent film version of *Godzilla* the creature is blessed with a nuclear fire-breath with which he blasts his foes. This is not strictly true to the original 1946 novel by Shohei Kawamura, however, in which the irradiated lizard kills enemies by way of radiation farts. A controversial anime from 1994 recreated the original but was quickly taken off the air when it was revealed the chief animator was colour-blind and the lizard appeared to be annihilating enemies with jets of liquid diarrhoea.

The Pacific Island of Manua (population 1,706) has a religion based around a farting deity. The island has a lush vegetation, its primary crop being protein-rich beans. In the religion's creation myth, the world is said to have been created after a celebration feast by the Creator, who farted out the earth and burped out the sun. Solar eclipses are taken as signs of celestial indigestion, and hurricanes viewed as manifestations of the food poisoning of the Creator, a superstition which really took hold after Hurricane Mandy hit in 1992, immediately after the island's first delivery of a supply of Imodium.

FARTING WORLD RECORDS

FIRST LIFE-SAVING FART

The only person ever known to have had his life saved by a fart was US airman Hank F. Peterson IX, who was stranded on a tropical island during the Second World War. Existing on a diet of beans and fruit, his anal iterations were so violent he took to lighting them at night in case he was rescued. This indeed happened in 1951 after six years on the island. However, the depraved sexual drawings he had made on the wide expanses of beach in his desperation were discovered the next day and led to his immediate imprisonment.

WORDS OF WINDSDOM

'The mind is everything. What you think, you become. And while you're pondering that I'm just going to, er, open this window a bit. Sorry. That is a stinker, isn't it.'

BUDDHA

Chirpy 1950s Preston North End left-back Harry Parfitt was well known for his changing-room antics, often performing pranks such as pouring curry powder in a teammate's jockstrap. On one occasion in 1957 he took a bet that he couldn't hide a golf ball up his backside for a full game. He performed this dubious feat in a fixture against Carlisle United but at the final whistle couldn't get the hidden obstacle out. Panicked, he dropped his shorts and bent over to facilitate deeper rummaging, upon which he farted, sending the golf ball far into the stand. The crowd were overjoyed and applauded rapturously but he was arrested for gross indecency and never played professionally again.

'If the yeti eats a monk, afterwards he speaks to heaven with his bottom.'
Tibetan proverb

✿ Certain varieties of German sausage have been marketed specifically to *exacerbate* farting. Many Germans consider the wind that follows a meal to be a pleasurable bonus, and have nicknamed it *der grumpfenblappenschticht*. In the late 1980s a company marketed a series of explosive new recipes, including the Burst Wurst (with the tagline that translated as 'Make your pants explode!'), Cursed Wurst ('It is like a demon is in your butthole'), Wurst Choice ('Your anus will be regretting your decision') and Hearse Wurst ('INSTANT DEATH GUARANTEED'). They proved popular among students.

✿ Considered by many to be an urban (or, more accurately, rural) myth, until the 1950s Welsh farting bread (*bara priddlyd arogl*) was presented each morning to hated English guests at B&Bs in the Monmouthshire area. It was a sturdy, heavily sugared and fruited loaf that was said to contain many illicit ingredients undetectable in the final product, including snot, pencil shavings or snipped-up grannies' underpants.

'If you fart at your wedding then you will stink up your whole life.'
Malay proverb

NATURAL WONDERS OF THE FARTING WORLD

The most farty substance in the world is the resin that seeps from the bababaluba tree common to north Venezuela – even inhaling the resin fumes can give humans violent flatulence. In fact, when close to a tonne of the resin seeped into the water supply after a landslide in 1969, a nearby town suffered the only ever recorded instance of mass TCF (total continuous flatulence), where victims are unable to stop farting. In honour of this event, the world's most skilful farters still gather in the town for the International Fartershop Quartet Contest.

WORDS OF WINDSDOM

'I have not told half of what I saw. And as for what I smelt . . . Jesus. I mean, you're better off not knowing mate, believe me.'
MARCO POLO

The first fart recorded in space was performed by Cosmo the Russian dog, on one of the first Soviet orbiting spacecrafts. The fart was heard by controllers in Russia and by radio hams all around the world. Many have speculated that it was an involuntary bodily expression of the wonder and awe that the animal felt staring out at the dark cosmos.

The dog died after many days of being trapped alone, eventually starving to death. You thought that was going to have a funny ending, didn't you? Nope.

> *'He who has itchy bum in night, in morning has smelly finger.'*
> **Chinese proverb**

The gusting mechanism of the steam train led many early users of the railway engine to dub it the 'farting carriage'. In fact, early graffiti was quite vociferous on the subject, referring to the railway engine as the 'guffing horses', the 'shit-breathing devil' and 'Aunt Elaine after cabbage'.

FARTING WORLD RECORDS

MOST DANGEROUS FART
Not all scientists believe that an asteroid killed the dinosaurs; some claim it was airborne toxicity caused by digestive gases from herbivores – meaning that their farting wiped out around half the living creatures on earth.

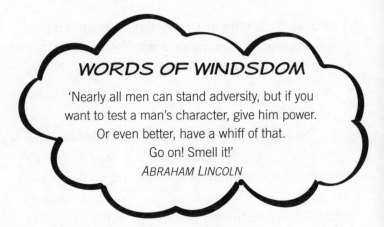

WORDS OF WINDSDOM

'Nearly all men can stand adversity, but if you
want to test a man's character, give him power.
Or even better, have a whiff of that.
Go on! Smell it!'
ABRAHAM LINCOLN

*'They that sow the wind, will reap the whirlwind. And
possibly have to change their trousers.'*
Proverb

Now a highly prized collector's item, the Farting
Chair is a 1954 piece by Dutch designer Jens de
Boikker. A lifelong martyr to flatulence, de Boikker
designed a box-like chair with deep comfortable
cushions and a funnel that led from the anus to a
hidden tank that could fill with unwanted flatus.
The design was hailed by the international design
community but sadly led to de Boikker's own death,
after a carpet spark caused by his rubber soled shoes
ignited the tank, sending flames up the spout and
causing the designer's torso to explode in the middle
of a meeting.

'If a bear farts in the woods, and there is no one to see it, does it make a sound?'
Siberian Buddhist proverb

The rarest fart in the natural world is that of the giant squid, of which there has only been one confirmed living sighting, by a trawler in the Indian Ocean in 1996. Having risen from its natural habitat in the far depths of the ocean, the squid was in great distress, resulting in a very large fart which one fisherman claimed to have caught in a jar. Giant squid fart gas became a highly profitable commodity on the black market, with many underground restaurants claiming to serve it as a starter salad (essentially as a mouthful of air on an empty plate) at an eye-watering premium. Apparently it smelled (or tasted) 'a bit like oyster'.

WORDS OF WINDSDOM

'We are all in the gutter. But some of us are looking at the stars. Yes, sorry, that was me. I've had a few.'
OSCAR WILDE

For designers working on the world's most advanced artificial intelligence robots, there is one unexpected job: creating digital farts with relatively accurate odour. Puzzled coders at the Masuhiro Foundation in Kyoto spent months being blindfolded and subjected to repulsive odours before turning their research into ones and zeroes over the course of months of eighteen-hour work days. The sequence of mass shootings in the area shortly afterwards was never formally linked to the project.

'When a puma farts in the night, an iguana kicks him in the balls.'
Peruvian proverb

CHOOSE
YOUR OWN
FARTVENTURE

2: THE JOB INTERVIEW

1. God, you hate job interviews. You really hate them. You hate them more than spiders, or Noel Edmonds. Possibly both of those things put together. But it's the only way. Get through by the skin of your teeth and you can stay in that job for ever and never have to do this again. After this everything will be fine, you promise yourself.

On the train on the way to the interview you suddenly realize that (having been too nervous to eat breakfast) you are catastrophically hungry.

You rummage around in your bag and to your surprise there's half a pulled-pork bagel in there. You're pretty sure it must be from the night before last, when you went out with your mates, and don't remember the end of the evening. Good times! Do you: a) wolf it down and proceed confidently to the interview with a full stomach, or b) decide that caution is the better option at such a crucial moment, and trust that you can grab something at the station when you arrive.

A) Go to number 2
B) Go to number 11

2. Hah. I like your style. Yum yum yum, pulled pork, pulled pork. Two days old or not, it hits the spot.

You get off at the station half an hour later, ignoring the toasted sandwich stall outside, and proceed confidently to the office, where you are asked to wait in reception. You sit down.

That's when a thought occurs to you. You *do* remember the end of the evening on Tuesday. You got a McDonald's, then a night bus. There was definitely no bagel shop involved. This revelation is accompanied by a slight churning sensation in your gut.

You haven't used this bag for weeks. Weeks and weeks. Maybe even since your last interview, and Christ almighty, that was before Christmas. It's nearly MAY. You break out in a chilly sweat. You're not due to be called for another five or so minutes. Is that enough time to get to the toilet and back? Impossible to tell. Do you a) ask where the loos are and sprint there or b) get a hold of your damn self! Are you three years old?

A) Go to number 3
B) Go to number 5

3. The nice reception lady is very helpful, and points to the toilets nearby. She simultaneously phones up to say that you're here. Apparently your interviewer will be down in 'a moment'. A frigging moment! What does that mean? Oh Jesus.

You're sweating profusely now, and shivering. You get in a cubicle and hang your head over the toilet bowl. Nothing happens. You've just ingested a writhing mass of angry bacteria the size of a cricket ball but it doesn't want to come out. You try sticking fingers down your throat but that never seems to work for you.

In trouserland, however, there are some violently unpleasant explosions. BAD THINGS ARE HAPPENING IN YOUR PANTS. Something, which feels not dissimilar to molten lead, is burrowing towards your bumhole. Do you a) hop on the loo and take care of it or b) decide it's too risky as you've only got 'a moment', splash water on your face and return to reception.

A) Go to number 4
B) Go to number 5

4. No sooner said than done. Pants down, botty on the john. Relief overwhelming. There's plenty of noise, but it's over swiftly. That's the main thing. Ah, god, that's better. You reach for the toilet roll but the holder's empty. Oh lordy. What to do?

The only piece of paper in your bag is your CV, which you have brought with you on the train so you could memorize the many falsehoods it contains. Owing to your distractingly ravenous hunger you have omitted to do this and now those lies are going to come back and bite you on your ragged arse! But do you want that already painful extremity to be also a stinky, squidgy, stinging one? HOW HAS YOUR LIFE COME TO THIS? Do you a) use the CV to effect the necessary task or b) decide it's too symbolic an act before going into an interview, pull up your trousers and put up with the discomfort, returning to reception?

A) Go to number 6
B) Go to number 5

5. Attempting to maintain a facade of control, you take a seat in reception.

Soon you are met by a friendly sort of chap, Jeremy, a couple of years older than you. You answer his remarks about the clement weather with honking grunts. In the interview room (thankfully only on the second floor) you meet the other interviewer, an avuncular sort of middle-aged, grey-haired gent called Graham. Of course he is. Probably a golfer. As you are unable to make much small talk, the interview immediately commences.

But your insides are killing you. Something's got to give. And there aren't many other contenders for the position of that something other than your arseflaps. However, these chairs are soft and deep and spongy, and covered in a light fabric. If your experience of long-haul flights has taught you anything, it's that chairs like this are mightily forgiving of a big old fart or three. Do you a) execute a cheeky sneaky fart to relieve the pressure and continue the interview with the benefit of your full attention, or b) ask to be excused and nip to the loo – surely these guys will understand, given the situation?

A) Go to number 7
B) Go to number 8

6. Okay, that was disgusting. But now it's over, you have a poo-smeared CV in your hands (and presumably a considerable amount of printer ink on your backside). You scrunch it up and are about to stick it in the lav when a horrible thought strikes you: what if it blocks the toilet? Then if it overflows the pages might flood out onto the floor, unfurling in the process. Someone could find them. It could end up ruining your chances of employment here. It could end up on Twitter! You could become the most famously unemployable person of all time! And have to put up with listening to your mum banging her new boyfriend in the next room for ever!

Do you a) ignore your own insane paranoia and flush the damn thing or b) remove this nagging doubt from your interview performance by scrunching the pages as tightly as possible and placing them at the bottom of your bag?

A) Go to number 8
B) Go to number 5

7. Having carefully manoeuvred your tush into the correct position (all the while nodding and smiling, and explaining about the marathon you ran for Cystic Fibrosis, as mentioned on your CV), you let fly. When it happens, though, your smile dies. You can see it in their faces, like lightning reflected off someone's glasses, how much your expression has suddenly changed. From joy to horror.

You haven't done a fart into their chair. You've shat yourself. And not just a bit. A pint. Something roughly akin to an armful of bubonic plague has exited your rear end. It's impossible to know how you should respond to this. There's no rulebook, to be honest. You stand up and say, 'Christ, I've shat myself!'

You waddle in your still-hot trousers to the loos, where you take stock for a while before someone throws their gym jogging bottoms over the stall for you to wear. Thanking them sincerely, you slip out of the building and wander home.

8. Flushing the loo, you feel an intense relief. You splash water on your face at the sinks and then proceed to your interview with young Jeremy and middle-aged Graham.

You've always hated interviews because deep down you don't understand them, you never know what to say. Now you have something to work against, however, you're at your best. Funny, sincere and concise, for half an hour you make a splendid account of yourself. Then you rise to leave, and remember that you're in the middle of contracting food poisoning. The room goes fuzzy for a moment, you nearly stagger. When you collect your thoughts, you realize you've audibly farted.

God DAMN it.

Do you a) make a joke of it. But that's a total shot in the dark – you reckon that men are probably fifty-fifty on being able to laugh at someone farting in front of them. Both Jeremy and Graham seem very nice and chilled. Or you could b) distract them somehow.

A) Go to number 9
B) Go to number 10

9. You pause, still slightly bending over, and look them both in the eye. Then you sigh, and put your hand to your head.

'It was going so well,' you say. 'Dammit!' You stand up fully, smiling ruefully. 'Unfortunately my bum and I disagree whether I'm suitable for this job. I'm so sorry about that.' Then you laugh, shake both men by the hand and leave.

Two days later you receive a phone call from Graham, saying he's delighted to offer you the job. You make a brief mention of the farting incident and he laughs out loud. 'You'll fit right in,' he chuckles. 'We'll sit you next to Brenda.'

You're overjoyed. Except about Brenda. She sounds unsavoury.

10. You leap to your feet. 'Wait a minute guys,' you say.

They both blink.

That's as far ahead as you'd thought. You scan your brain desperately, and all you come up with is to a) make up something to do with the window cleaner (who's just winched himself into sight outside the window) or b) to pretend you're part of a hidden-camera TV show. They're both shit ideas. BUT THERE'S NO TIME! Which do you choose?

A) Go to number 19
B) Go to number 20

11. The lack of food distraction on the train allows you time to study the CV you sent them (and memorize its plethora of terrible lies – according to which you're some sort of cross between Mohatma Gandhi and Indiana Jones). Plus, no sooner do you arrive than you spot a toasted-sandwich seller stall outside. Brilliant! Quick, cheap and effective. You eat one and arrive at the interview very pleased with your preparation.

You are interviewed by Jeremy, a youngish bloke, and Graham, a friendly middle-aged guy. The interview starts well.

However, eating that toasty after such a long break has got your digestive system working.

You're only five minutes through your first answer when suddenly the need to fart is there. It blocks out all other thoughts. Your insides must be in a worse condition than you thought. You cough to distract yourself from the pain, and unfortunately that immediately proves a bad mistake. You fart with the sound of an accelerating motorbike. This is now a worst-case scenario. Do you a) make up some total bullshit to try and distract the two men, b) freak out and blame one of them or c) apologize?

A) Go to number 12
B) Go to number 13
C) Go to number 14

12. 'Do you know what?' you say in your most suave voice, 'I think I'd like to answer that last question with a little exercise.'

Okay. You're going with this. You don't know where you're going, but you are going.

'If you would stand up,' you say to them. 'This is based on a Japanese study I read concerning preconceptions in the workplace.' The two interviewers are clearly impressed. In fact, you're rather impressed as well. You reckon if you can pull this off, you've got the job for sure. All you've got to do is improvise a meaningful test from Japan that says something about something vaguely to do with work. How hard can that be? You're about to find out. Should you a) do a Japanese accent and speak in broken English while carrying out the test or b) not?

A) You're insane. You deserve everything that's coming to you. You try it for about a second and then realize it's wildly inappropriate. Go to number 15

B) Of course not. Go to number 15

13. You're really tired and you don't want the job. Plus you really need to fart a whole lot more.

You cover your face with your hands and then do a full-on Gary Oldman-from-*Leon* meltdown.

'Could I ASK YOU,' you shriek operatically, trembling, 'Not to break wind in my BLOODY INTERVIEW? WOULD THAT BE OKAY WITH YOU GUYS?'

They stare at you, stunned.

There's a golf club mounted on the office wall (obviously Graham's) and you momentarily consider taking it down and smashing some stuff up. But the frustration and humiliation is already out of your system. It feels good yelling that loudly.

'I'll see myself out,' you mutter over your shoulder.

Once you've strolled out of sight, you sprint for freedom. You are rather cheerful for the rest of the day. But still jobless and, let's be frank, a dickhead.

14. 'I'm so incredibly sorry,' you say. The two men are put out to say the least. You give a stiff performance for the rest of the interview and receive a rejection letter two days later.

15. Okay. So, you get the two guys to stand up. That seems a good start. Then you get Graham to close his eyes. Fuckity fuck, what next? Okay, okay. You open the door to the broom cupboard in the corner of the room.

'Right,' you say. 'When you hear this door close, Graham, I want you to open your eyes. Then decide which of us you think is in the cupboard.'

For some reason you think it's important that it's you who's in the cupboard. So you position Jeremy standing behind Graham where he can't be seen, motion him to be silent and step inside the cupboard. Closing the door, you are folded into welcoming velvety darkness. To which your body responds by telling you in no uncertain terms that it needs to fart again, with even more severity than before. Do you a) give in to this possibly suicidal desire or b) repress it, risking something even worse?

A) Go to number 16
B) Go to number 17

16. Surely a victimless crime! You're already acing the interview. Who could blame you if you want to get rid of another potential obstacle by farting in a broom cupboard? No one! That's who!

After doing the dirty deed, you emerge from the closet to find Graham rather tickled by your little experiment.

'Interesting,' he says. 'Interesting. Let's swap places. You close your eyes.'

Shit.

'No,' you say. 'It only works once.'

'Okay Jeremy, you close your eyes.' No sooner has the young man done this than Graham madly leaps for the cupboard.

Well, it looks like your jig is up. Do you a) admit that you farted in the cupboard or b) infuriated that he's not doing what you want, wrestle him to the ground?

A) Go to number 17
B) Go to number 18

17. 'I farted in there!' you blurt. Graham stops in his tracks.

Both men burst out laughing. To your astonishment, they assume you're joking. In fact, they both assume that whatever this test is, they're getting it wrong and you were being nice by making them stop the test now rather than make fools of themselves.

It seems that, in some way, you've shown yourself to be a good sort, a team player. A fitter-inner. No answer you give from this point on can do anything but please them inordinately.

Two days later you are given the job. You end up working there for eighteen years. Then you have a mental breakdown and insist that you've been abducted by aliens. But that's unrelated. In the short term, the fart ruse worked nicely.

18. Stupid fat bastard. You hit him hard around the middle with a nicely aimed rugby tackle and wrestle him to the floor. The fact that he wriggles madly, still trying to get to the broom cupboard, infuriates you further and you pop him one on the jaw. Jeremy's on your back now, but because you're hunched over pummelling Graham, it's easy to fling him over your shoulder. He hits the wall upside down and slumps.

You can hear footsteps.

You scurry to the door and sneak out, half running to the lift. Take the stairs, you decide. You find an abandoned floor three storeys above, all loose wires and missing ceiling tiles. Crawling to the most distant corner you stay there for four or five hours. Until the heat has died down. You sleep a bit. When you wake, it's dark. You cry softly, curled in a ball. You look out the windows down at the Midlands city where you live. Look at the world. It's at your fingertips. All you have to do is reach out and take it. You break wind extremely loudly.

19. 'I'm sorry guys,' you say sternly, 'is this some sort of test?'

They both stare at you uncomprehending.

'That guy, the window cleaner,' you say, 'was he supposed to do that?'

'Do what?' Graham asks.

'He was being deliberately off-putting,' you say.

'I'm so sorry,' says Graham. He gestures angrily at the window, where the innocent cleaner is getting on with his job.

'Allow me,' you say.

You step up to the window and knock sharply on it. At last there's a breath of air in the room as the cleaner opens the window. Too late, however, to save you from your own bottom. You let one go when you stood up and Graham and Jeremy look disgusted. Knowing this charade is over, you quietly climb up through the window and out onto the gantry beside the window cleaner. Then you pull the window closed behind you.

'You won't believe this, but it's a challenge for charity,' you explain cheerfully. 'If I can commandeer a window cleaner's lift and ride it to the ground, I'll make a grand for kids.'

'But we're only on the second floor,' he replies, nonplussed.

'Yup.' You nod enthusiastically.

'Okay whatever,' says the guy. When you reach the ground you sprint off into the distance with a yelled 'cheers mate' over your shoulder.

20. 'You're not going to believe this, guys,' you say, standing and adopting what you think of as a TV voice, 'but you guys are on camera right now.'

They don't believe you.

'Don't believe me?' you ask rhetorically. 'Well, what you don't know is that there are cameras in three places around the room. You see, we're making a new show where we will put people through embarrassing situations and capture their reactions on film. Like farting in an interview! My name is Brent Stambleblam, I'm the presenter. And you just got Stambleblam-bammed!' Keep going, keep going, for god's sake.

'My assistant Mandy will be through in a minute to get you to sign release forms. But I'm guessing you'll be all right with that? Sure you will. Okay guys, I'm out of here. Be safe. And by the way, that's a real guy's CV that we used to get this interview. So it would be sweet if you could put him forward for any other jobs that are going in your corporation. Okay. Time out. Latey-lates.' You snap your fingers twice with both hands and then waltz out of the room backwards firing finger-guns at the two guys until you're out of sight, although unfortunately that doesn't happen until after you've fallen over an empty water-cooler bottle.

Weirdly, you do get a call from the HR department a few months later, when you still haven't landed a job. On the back of it you temp for three weeks in the marketing department. It's a shit job, but there you meet Jessica, with whom you now have a beautiful baby son.

SCENARIOS
11–15

(ADVANCED)

SURVIVAL SCENARIO 11: AFTER TAKING A VOW OF SILENCE

Subject H has been a Carthusian monk for more than thirty years, and in that time his love for the saviour hasn't missed a single heartbeat. Despite some misgivings about the constant silence thing, he's definitely on board with the fact that God's a terrific guy. Or woman. JOKES! He's definitely a man.

Subject H has filled his considerable spare time by writing slash fiction. He started off doing some pretty innocent stuff but he rapidly noticed that people on the internet crave filth. Difficult though, as a monk, to write with authority on the subject. So he has instead spent a few years peopling the sprawling online world of *Fifty Shades of Grey* fan-fic with nice people who make increasingly elaborate excuses not to touch each other. And to his surprise it turns out that abstinence is like a rare delicacy to these jaded palates. Readers have taken to it in droves and there are now offers of hard cash on the table from publishers.

How to bring up the subject with the **Abbot**, though? **Subject H** has decided to approach him with a written letter at the only time he's visible – at dinner, in front of everyone.

He's only three feet away when for the first time he can remember in his entire adult life he uncontrollably breaks wind. It is LOUD, like a gunshot at first, then it trails away. Everyone stares at him.

WHAT DOES SUBJECT H DO?

Solution A (Sane)

Farting isn't disallowed under the rules of the Order. It's frowned upon, for sure. But then what isn't?

As **Subject H** stands there, enveloped with his own waft, he realizes that his plan of getting sanctioned to publish a book of *Fifty Shades of Grey* fan-fiction always had a pretty much 100 per cent chance of failure. He quickly stuffs the letter back in his pocket. But that leaves him standing, caught in front of the top table diners with one arm and one leg stretching forward. It is a silly pose.

Not knowing any other way to get out of this position, **Subject H** starts to dance. Acting on pure instinct, he does a little tap dance based on the old Fred Astaire and Ginger Rogers movies he used to love. What was his favourite one, with that number in the snow? *Swing Time?* When he looks up he is astonished to find that three other monks have fallen in step behind him. Then when he turns with a flourish he sees another group of five more are dancing behind those three!

To **Subject H**'s surprise, the **Abbot** looks ecstatic. And **Subject H** realizes that there is, of course, no law against dancing in the monastery. Dancing, in fact, is a way of praising some of God's most wonderful creations: legs, musical time and Ginger Rogers. Unwittingly, **Subject H** has created something that will become an after-dinner routine for the monks for many years to come, and even bring the monastery national fame as the winner of a TV talent show – albeit long after he has left in disgrace. And long after anyone (including himself) can remember the fart.

Solution B (Risky)

Subject H: Oh, bollocks.

OH NO. Did he just speak? It slipped out before he has a chance to think. The room goes silent. *More* silent. **Subject H** glances furtively over his shoulder to see if anyone heard.

OF COURSE they heard. What did he think was going to mask the sound of his voice? Two guys chatting about the football?

Subject H feels a large number of emotions all at once. Relief. Wow, it's so amazing to hear his own voice. And to find out he's still got one! Then, simultaneously, a crushing wave of guilt. Has anyone ever been more busted than this, since they found Guy Fawkes in the big room directly beneath parliament with all the gunpowder and the box of matches?

Subject H (sheepishly): Well, at least I didn't say 'Oh Jesus'. You've got to give me that.

More silence. *Christ!*

Subject H: Sheesh, tough crowd.

Still nothing. To imagine you'd find such an unforgiving audience in a Christian place.

Subject H: Well who put a stick up *your* butts? Huh? Jesus? You mean the one that *doesn't exist*?

Okay. Now he knows he took it too far. He's drunk on the freedom of being able to talk. He makes it to the door just as he is grabbed and dragged out by three ashen-faced monks. He can't stop grinning and babbling, even though he can't remember why it was he started speaking anyway.

The last traces of the fart have vanished.

Solution C (Kamikaze)

Uh-oh. Defcon 5.

Farting in front of the **Abbot** has got to be a punishable offence. And it's roly-poly Wednesday today. He's buggered if he's missing out on pudding. So he'll have to fake it up big-time. Pretend he's been possessed. They can exorcise him this afternoon then he'll make sure they know he's okay by bedtime and can ask for some left-over dessert.

He starts to hiss and spit.

Subject H (demon voice): Your daughter sucks cocks in Hell!

He instantly wonders whether he should have quoted directly from *The Exorcist*. Firstly because that's definitely not a film they're supposed to have seen. But more importantly, to anyone who *has* seen the film that does sound a little bit like what someone would say who's pretending they're possessed, not like what a demon might come out with of its own accord.

Still, too late to go back now.

Subject H starts rolling his eyes and concentrating on trying to make foam come out of his mouth. Infuriatingly, this is more difficult than he feels it ought to be.

No one approaches him. Time to step it up a gear.

He begins to gargle as loudly as he can and writhe on the floor. He is quickly gathered up and taken to the infirmary, slapped, splashed with water, prayed for, and eventually left to snooze.

All memory of the fart has disappeared. Along with his dreams of being a published author.

WORDS OF WINDSDOM

'When I reached the bar at the Drones club, I reacquainted myself with Whiffles, Pongo and Old Spludger. But then I always get terrible wind after kedgeree for breakfast. Afterwards I apologized to everyone present. Perhaps it is weird to name one's farts, after all.'

P. G. WODEHOUSE

SURVIVAL SCENARIO 12: WHILE AT AN EDITORIAL LUNCH ABOUT THIS BOOK

Subject B is the author of this book. He looks exactly as you would expect – a furtive, soiled, ingratiating creep in his mid-thirties who somehow seems to sit with a limp. The sort of creature who slides from a room leaving an aroma that makes other men entering it sniff themselves in alarm. He sits at the restaurant table twitching nervously, simpering at each man who passes his table, assuming that he is the book's editor, who he is about to meet for the first time. Finally the **Editor**, a forthright and business-like individual, arrives, glancing at his watch. He has places to be and frankly resents the obligation of eating lunch with someone so unimportant – it is an oversight on his part that he did not make an excuse in time.

Editor: You must be—

Subject B nods eagerly. They shake hands and the **Editor** sits.

As **Subject B**'s eyes flit hungrily over the menu the **Editor** takes a sidelong glance at the author, and has to repress his disgust. Well, someone has to write the books, he supposes. What stone did this one crawl out from beneath?

Subject B: So, how are . . . how are you . . .

Editor (sighing): One gets by. (To the waiter.) I shall have a mineral water to start. And a green salad.

Subject B (who has not seen the waiter approaching): Oh – I – may I have a glass of – wine . . . ?

Editor: I can't stop you.

Subject B (nodding furiously): A bad idea, bad idea. Water. Water for me. And ah – er – perhaps the steak . . . the prawns . . . ?

He glances nervously at the **Editor**, who is studying his fingernails through hooded eyelids.

Subject B (gulps): Green salad would be . . . (swallows a retch, covering mouth with back of hand) marvellous, thank you.

Editor: Now let's get something straight. Do you know what authors are?

Subject B narrows his eyes, trying to think of the required answer. He shakes his head.

Editor: Worms. They are worms.

Subject B: Because they . . . nourish, humbly . . . ?

Editor: Because they are the lowest of the low,

and when they rear their ugly heads they should be crushed. Like mice.

Subject B: Not worms?

Editor: No. Like Mice.

Things are going less well even than **Subject B** could have predicted – and he always predicts things will go very badly indeed (he is usually correct).

At this moment, however, he is for once proved wrong – because things *do* get worse, as he violently breaks wind.

WHAT DOES SUBJECT B DO?

Solution A (Sane)

Subject B is the author of a book about farts. Therefore the only thing we can tell about him for sure is that he has no self-respect. Shocked – terrified even – at the implications of this fart for his own career, he leaps up and sprints from the table with a muttered excuse.

In the gents **Subject B** slams the cubicle door shut behind him. But no sooner has he stepped back into the restaurant than he is struck by another even stronger attack of wind. He bursts through a fire exit door, twitching violently and nervously scratching his eczema. Just when he thinks he's got rid of the smell another one rips uncontrollably through him, louder and smellier than before. *Damn* those pound-shop frankfurters! He windmills furiously at his bottom area with his arms to get rid of the smell, then decides it would be quicker to pull down his trousers.

In the act of yanking his stained grey jogging bottoms to his knees, **Subject B** skids in a puddle, then trips. Unable to stop himself, he sprawls into the road face-first and his head falls under the wheel of an oncoming lorry, where it is instantly crushed. Naturally by the time that the **Editor** is apprised of the facts the fart smell has already been quite forgotten.

Solution B (Risky)

Subject B can't mess this lunch up – if he can impress the **Editor**, who knows what might come of it? He refuses to be plunged back into obscurity. Not another winter writing catalogue copy for local garden centres. A little old chap dining alone on the table next to them gives **Subject B** hope.

Subject B: WHAT A REVOLTING SMELL. I daresay you are the author of that repulsive odour, sir. I demand an apology.

Old Man: A . . . pardon?

Subject B: I SAID AN APOLOGY. At once!

Old Man: Well, I . . .

Subject B: Clearly we shall have to take this matter outside!

Old Man: I . . . no, I . . . please . . .

Editor (somewhat shaken): I say, Subject B, settle down old chap?

Subject B: Well, really!

Subject B is reluctantly persuaded back to his seat having bestowed his gracious forgiveness on the little old man.

Editor: I can see I was wrong about you, Subject B. I expected you would be like all the other authors. A cowardly wretch. But it seems you have a rare mettle. There is a certain project I have been waiting to find the right author for. Bound to turn into a sequence of bestsellers, film rights sure to sell. Millions await. Let me tell you about it . . .

Subject B: I'm all ears, my dear fellow.

Solution C (Kamikaze)

The **Editor** is not fooled for a moment by the revolting odour. He casts a suspicious and frankly withering gaze upon his unkempt author. **Subject B** perceives that now is his time to act.

Subject B (urbanely): Revolting smell. I know it well.

Editor: Yes. From your own posterior, you ANIMAL.

Subject B (chuckles): Not at all. That's the smell of a bottle of Andalucian sherry matured in smoked oak casks for that single week too long, which has made it spoil.

The **Editor**, startled, sniffs the air. Then he sits up, and looks at **Subject B** as if for the first time.

Editor: Perhaps you're right. That takes me back to Seville in 92. On a little jaunt with William Boyd, Kingsley Amis. A. S. Byatt even turned up for a few days. Phew, we had some hangovers . . .

Subject B: Ah. But the industry has changed.

Editor: Changed? It's unrecognisable! Sometimes I dream of settling down to write the old memoirs, perhaps retire to the villa in Umbria . . .

Subject B: Nonsense. You're in the prime of life!

Editor: Too kind, Subject B, too kind. A thrusting young man's game though, I fear. If only I could be sure of handing over the business to someone with an ounce of sense . . . But of course! *You* must do it. I'll phone the contracts department and have the papers sorted out at once. There's the matter of a salary – a couple of hundred thou ought to do?

They high-five. Neither of them takes any notice of the still-lingering smell.

SURVIVAL SCENARIO 13: WHILE PLAYING A CORPSE ON STAGE

Subject F's had glamorous jobs (a pretty mum in a yoghurt advert) and had fun on deliberately anti-glamour ones (a witch on a kids' TV show). But she flunked fifteen TV auditions in a row, and now she's on a touring production of an Agatha Christie mystery, giving the performance of her life as a dead body. She is convinced she makes a pretty corpse. But it is still a less-than-a-hundred-per-cent-glamorous job.

Rufus, playing the Colonel, has been droning on for some time about the dubious morality of 'this girl' who has been found dead in his scullery. A combination of outdated gender politics, awkward dialogue, the crummy venue, plus the admirable but vain efforts of her poor cast-mates are too much. All of it, together, makes **Subject F** want to giggle.

But she refuses to giggle. Professional discipline!

However, she is caught unawares by the effect that professional discipline, applied at one end, has on the other. All of a sudden **Subject F** lets out a buttsqueak. Sharp, high-pitched, unmistakably audible to everyone from the front row up to the cheapest seats.

Oh shit.

WHAT DOES SUBJECT F DO?

Solution A (Sane)

Subject F goes rigid. She genuinely can't think what to do. Please, someone, do something!

Then (peeping through her closed eyes) she catches sight of **Rufus**, the terrible old ham. She can see the look of frank disgust on his face. At the same time as this, he spots the twitching at the corner of her mouth and realizes she's trying not to laugh. Well, he thinks, why not play along.

Rufus: They never tell you that corpses do that, do they? Always comes as a shock. (Then adds wistfully) That dead people should be so rude . . .

He then carries on with his speech exactly as before. This unexpected interlude is, it turns out, perfectly timed. After a boozy interval at the bar, it gets a genuine laugh from the weary audience. This, in turn, gives the cast's performance a sudden zest, a little wind in their sails.

The positive audience reaction puts everyone on good terms with each other, and makes most of the cast firm friends. **Subject F** will have a final catch-up with the last surviving cast member sixty years later, in 2075, when they both play the grandparents in a new sitcom set within the Marvel-DC Studios Entertainment Multiverse™, which encompasses the entirety of Denmark. By then neither of them can remember the fart. But then, they can hardly remember anything.

Solution B (Risky)

The matter of what to do next is taken immediately out of **Subject F**'s hands. Unbeknownst to her, **Rufus** has in fact just been dumped by his boyfriend. He's a man on the edge. This fart awakens in him a terrible realisation of where his life is really 'at'. And so startled is he that in response he has no option but to laugh.

Rufus: She's not dead! She's faking! Look, she's laughing!

Well of course she's laughing. She's really *corpsing* now, thanks to him. And some of the audience are laughing too, heartily, while the rest remain silent.

Also, now that he's said that, not only the seriousness of the play but the plot too are both doomed.

Subject F: Yes! You have caught me out this time!

Rufus (at the top of his voice): Fiend! She lives! The dead bitch is alive! Kill her!

He chases her off stage – she daintily runs ahead of him, yelping. As they go into the wings, they stand there, breathing hard. **Rufus** turns and walks back on stage.

Rufus (to the audience): This flimsy veil, reality. So easily punctured. Our corpse returns . . .

Subject F knows her cue and walks solemnly back to the couch where she lies and remains still. The play takes off again from mid-speech.

Most of the middle-class audience is vaguely convinced that what they've just seen is an intentional part of the play, in a clever way that they don't quite understand. They definitely don't like it, but they're dimly aware that if they voice their disapproval they might become somehow famous for their ignorance. Like the crowd who didn't like Stravinsky's *The Rite of Spring* at its debut. They remain angrily silent and afterwards never speak about it again. When the cast gather afterwards for the firing of their lives they discover the director was in the pub all along and hasn't seen a thing. So they go off to join him.

Solution C (Kamikaze)

Subject F sits up slowly. All the other actors freeze. She looks at the audience.

The audience look at her. She looks at **Rufus**. He is looking a tad confused. He is trapped mid-pause.

She looks back at the audience again. The time to act is now . . . She assumes that she's going to be fired for farting loudly on stage. Chances are she'll be known for it in acting circles. Might never work again. Could have to move back to Pontypridd. No. Anything but that.

She pops a boob out.

Then the other.

Then she pops them back in. Lies down again. Remains still.

Rufus blinks, his eyebrows wobble slightly.

Rufus: As I was saying . . .

Might as well be hung for a sheep as a lamb, is

Subject F's logic. Besides, no one ever minds an actress getting her waps out. It's positively encouraged. Has she just discovered a real-life version of the mind-wiping stick from *Men in Black*? Well, no one in the audience is thinking about the fart, that's for sure.

WORDS OF WINDSDOM

'Reports of my death are greatly exaggerated. Although it was touch and go there for a while because that was one hell of a strong vindaloo. Wow, is my arse ragged.'
MARK TWAIN

SURVIVAL SCENARIO 14: WHILE AT A FUNERAL

Someone from the office had to come along and **Subject Z** drew the short straw. But **Subject Z** has two very good reasons for being pissed off about being at this funeral. Firstly, he's had to take the day off work unpaid, owing to him slightly messing up the monthly holiday allocation. Secondly, it's the funeral of Clive Holland, a former colleague who could best be described as a fat, unpleasant moron.

And I mean *best* described. A man who only ever used his brain to work out what would be the most moronic and unpleasant thing to do. And who only expended energy in his efforts to get fatter. Now he's dead, and a bunch of people are gathered in this cold-arse graveyard trying to pretend to give a damn.

A sucker for punishment, **Subject Z** even agreed to come to the graveside. He's been standing here for twenty-five minutes, and the **Priest** has only just arrived.

It's as **Subject Z** stands with his gloved hands behind him in the frosty morning air and ignoring the words of the **Priest**, that he is suddenly and inescapably assailed by an 'attack of wind'. He has achieved a state of such perfect boredom and grumpiness that the fart catches him unawares, ripping out of him like a rocket. There is no question that everyone must have heard it.

WHAT DOES SUBJECT Z DO?

Solution A (Sane)

Not just for his own sake, but for the close friends and relatives present, **Subject Z** needs to make a post-fart diversion. He must make this right.

So before the ringing sound of the fart has died away, and as the startled crows on the nearby tree are still unfurling their wings, he pushes past the two people in front of him by the graveside and falls to his knees. He raises his face to the sky and bellows.

Subject Z: WHY? Why did it have to happen? Why, Lord? WHY?

Priest (looking a bit put out): Is there a doctor here?

Subject Z hears someone muttering from the back of the group. Instead of being patted on the back, told to keep his chin up and bear it, and perhaps having his tears dabbed away by a pretty girl's handkerchief, everyone has pulled back from the grave to give him a wide berth.

As **Subject Z** stares up at the sky, engrossed in his performance, he doesn't see Clive's brother stealing up behind him. If Clive was the abominable prototype of an unpleasant moron, **Terry** is very much the finished model. Bigger, uglier, crueller.

Terry fixes **Subject Z** with a smack across the back of the head that knocks him clean out and then, with practised smoothness, catches his falling body. As he drags **Subject Z** away, he tells the **Priest** to go on with the service.

Later, **Subject Z** will wake up lying on the sarcophagus of a Dr Phelps, who died in 1873. Like everyone in the funeral party, he will have no memory of the fart. Nor will he have any knowledge of who he is or how he got here.

WORDS OF WINDSDOM

'Hell is other people's bottom smell. That was my original quote. I hate it when that gets misquoted as just "other people". Which it does all the time. JESUS.'

JEAN-PAUL SARTRE

Solution B (Risky)

If **Subject Z** loathes one thing, it is silent recrimination. Having dealt the fart, he cannot bear to stand around while people blame him for it, hate him for it. No – he can't and won't endure it.

'Oops, that's my signal,' says **Subject Z** breezily, on the retort that sounds from his trousers. He wiggles through the mourners to the graveside. There is instantly a moment of unease. Everyone is unsure what this remark might mean, or if they heard it right.

'Okay guys,' he says, smiling, 'now this is going to come as a leeetle bit of a surprise, but as some of us know, in the last two years Clive took up magic. And he never did things by half. Or should I say, never *does* things by half. Because Clive's great ambition was one day to be a witness to his own funeral. And today he has done it, ladies and gentlemen!'

Most of the mourners have turned their eyes away in horror. Some are fiddling with their phones, either to call the police or start filming with their cameras. Unbowed by this reception, **Subject Z** leaps down onto the coffin. He lands with a horrible thump and squeak as his wet feet skid slightly on the polished lid.

Subject Z: Fear not, my chubby friend! For you are shortly to be reborn like a fat Lazarus! Knock, Clive! Knock! Show everyone here that you are really alive!

Several people are now loudly sobbing. It occurs to him in this moment that the one thing he would need for this subterfuge to work is for Clive to be not dead. This suddenly gives him pause and he leaves off thumping the coffin long enough to be punched in the face by Clive's brother **Terry** and rendered unconscious. Afterwards no one has any memory of a fart.

Solution C (Kamikaze)

No sooner has the fart rung out from his pants than **Subject Z** screams. He must divert attention from his fart.

Subject Z: A ghost! Over there!

Everyone freezes. Who the hell screams something at a funeral? **Subject Z** knows that the worst thing he can do right now is back down.

Subject Z: Right there! Behind that stone! I saw it!

A male relative takes a step forward and puts his hand on **Subject Z**'s arm.

Male relative: You all right? This is . . . This is a funeral, mate.

Subject Z: What are you saying? That I'm a liar? That I'm *insane*? I'll *show* you. It was over here . . .

He scampers off excitedly. By the time the relative catches up with him, he is breathing hard and whispering under his breath.

Male relative (appearing round a corner): Okay, what was it that you—

Subject Z has taken off his patent leather shoe and smacks the poor guy round the head, knocking him clean out. Then he runs off in the opposite direction to Clive's grave, screaming at the top of his lungs and flapping his arms until he's out of sight.

Two years later he is in a gay bar when he happens across **Terry**, Clive's brother. Who punches him in the face.

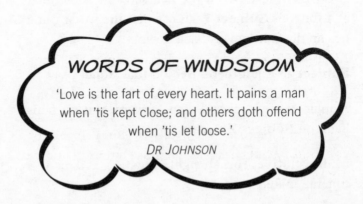

WORDS OF WINDSDOM

'Love is the fart of every heart. It pains a man when 'tis kept close; and others doth offend when 'tis let loose.'
DR JOHNSON

SURVIVAL SCENARIO 15: WHILE BEING ABDUCTED BY ALIENS

Her taxi's rammed in hideous traffic and **Subject Y** is trying to explain over her BlackBerry to her stultifyingly unintelligent new assistant how to send out a contract request form. Then there's a blinding orange light, some brief pain, and what feels like an extraordinarily long sleep, before she wakes up in a white circular room. She assumes she's been in an accident. Until the aliens walk in.

The aliens are more ugly than she would have expected (all tubes and pus), but she keeps this to herself.

Alien #1: She is repulsed by us physically. From her brainwaves.

Subject Y: No, no, I . . .

Alien #2: She's no bloody oil painting.

Alien #3: Guys. Can we focus? This is a moment. (Clears throat-like tubes, with rasping sound.) Earthling Creature, we bring welcome from the Zallamus Nebula. You are our chosen representative from Earth.

Subject Y: Oh. Hello.

Alien #1: Is that all she can say?

A great moment – the first meeting of two galactic civilisations. What might come of this union? What will they make of our culture? Shakespeare should go down a treat but how to explain Donald Trump? The nerves of the occasion overcome **Subject Y** and she is presently betrayed by the 'naked' broccolini and soy bean salad she had for lunch. A parp escapes her trouser department.

WHAT DOES SUBJECT Y DO?

Solution A (Sane)

If ever there's a time to get away with a fart, it's when meeting creatures from another planet. **Subject Y** is the sort of woman who eats raw broccoli for lunch – she pretty much *always* wants to fart. The slightly pained expression she constantly wears is almost entirely down to that. And her first husband. But mostly that. So this is a glorious new beginning for her. These . . . these things, for all she knows, have no notion of smell. They might have fifteen extra senses which humans lack. But for once in her life she could be in a social situation where she doesn't even have to style it out – just pretend it never happened!

Subject Y: Delighted to meet you. On behalf of the citizens of Planet Earth, I say. . . Howdy!

Alien #3: 'Howdy?'

Alien #2: I told you we should have chosen Alan Yentob.

Alien #1: WHAT IS THAT FUCKING SMELL?

Subject Y: What smell? I mean, er – what's a smell?

The three aliens go into spasm. They contort and gyrate, almost as though they are dancing.

Aliens #1-3: Aaargh, ow, make it stop!

Subject Y is starting to have misgivings about her handling of the situation. But she's always been one to stick to a story once she's chosen it.

Subject Y: This smell thing you speak of, describe it to me. Does it cause you pleasure or pain?

Alien #1: Would you get a load of the wide-eyed innocence on this one!

Alien #2: 'This smell thing you speak of'? Look at us – all the tubes. We are MADE of noses.

Alien #3 (reaching forward with one of his tubes to press a button on the console): Okay, that's enough, sweetheart.

Subject Y: Great. Nice to see sexism thrives elsewhere in the solar s—

There is a blinding flash, and **Subject Y** appears to be back on Earth, in her cab again. Still in Goodge Street. The cabbie is still leaning on his horn. She blinks, and makes a note on her tablet to go to the doctor very soon. Then she taps on the cabbie's plastic screen.

Subject Y: Who is Alan Yentob?

Cabbie: Don't get me fucking started.

Back in the spaceship, **Alien #3** is regretting his choice. Perhaps the next solar system along will be a better place to go and start a colony. He decides to spare these humans their smelly little lives. The craft zips into space.

Solution B (Risky)

If **Subject Y** has learned anything from being a successful businesswoman it's that with the smallest amount of effort you can take charge of a social situation. Until proven otherwise she will assume this applies to aliens as well.

First order of business: get everyone present away from the smelly scene of the crime.

Subject Y: How FASCINATING to meet you all. And what a wonderful craft . . .

She strides to the back of the large white room, where there is a door. To her pleasure it swishes automatically back to reveal the room behind.

Alien #1: Oh, don't worry about all that.

Alien #2: It's just a dusty old cloakroom, I wouldn't pay any attention . . .

Subject Y is surrounded by an arsenal of very enormous and terrifying weapons. She turns to look up at a large map of the solar system – each of the planets is marked through with a giant red cross. Earth, however, is circled with several arrows pointing towards it. Next to the arrows on the map is a crude picture of one of the aliens, flinging a human into his gaping mouth, while he rubs his stomach.

Subject Y turns to look at the three aliens, who are all looking slightly abashed.

Alien #3 (the first to recover): Now, I agree, unless you know what you're looking at, that could *seem* bad.

Subject Y (pointing at a gleaming metallic surgeon's table above which are poised a dozen gleaming dissection instruments): So this is all innocent, I take it, part of the normal civilisation-greeting procedure . . .

Alien #1: Looks uncomfy, I grant you, but it's all above board . . . don't get the wrong impression!

Subject Y doesn't say anything right away, but instead leaps up onto a giant tank-like assault vehicle and hopping in the seat and grabbing the joystick, trains a cannon on the aliens' arses.

Alien #2: Don't do anything you might–oh shit—

Subject Y blasts them all away. It's deeply satisfying. Two days later she steers the craft to land on the Siberian plains. The technology found therein cures the energy shortage and fuels a hundred thousand years of peace on Earth. So that's nice. Isn't it?

Solution C (Kamikaze)

Having flounced from the room as in Solution B, and discovered the Destruction Chamber, **Subject Y** pauses. Beneath her, through an observation panel, hangs the green planet. Through the glass she can see multi-various large-snouted weapons primed and pointing down at Earth's sensitive skin.

Earth. What is it good for, **Subject Y** asks herself? Shakespeare, yes. And sushi. Bob Dylan. Some people would say Bill Hicks, even though Doug Stanhope is still alive and better. The Temple of the Golden Pavilion at Kyoto. Jelly babies . . .

Yet, any world that contains **Subject Y**'s first husband is an inherently evil and unstable place. And any world that contains her *second* husband will be largely unaffected by his benign and slightly pointless presence. They don't balance each other out.

Subject Y reaches a sudden soaring epiphany, and a simultaneous sense of freedom.

Subject Y: I don't know how you knew I was the only human who was immune. Did you have some sort of detector?

Alien #2: Yawn. Whatever. Proceed with invasion . . .

Alien #1: Wait a flipping minute, Julian . . .

Alien #3: Are you saying, young lady, that the populace is infected?

Subject Y: You mean you didn't KNOW? What are you, CRAZY? This is the plague planet! I am the only non-infected person out of seven billion! You're going to toast the place right now, right?

Aliens #1-3 seem dubious. At length, after much persuasion, the aliens nuke Planet Earth to an orange husk. They then proceed on their intergalactic travels, with the last remaining human aboard, who will teach future generations of cute little aliens a slightly tendentious history of Earth that paints her in an entirely flattering light. Bongo!

FARTERS OF
STAGE AND
SCREEN

Many fans of the Lord of the Rings trilogy don't realize that, before his death in 1972, Professor Tolkien had been working on a prequel novel based on the life of Gimli the Dwarf. In the novel, Gimli was trapped in a travelling circus where he was beaten with straps of unicorn hide and forced to fart for audiences of hobbits. In the end he died miserably in a ditch, aged just seventeen, which obviously made a nonsense of the Lord of the Rings novels. The first draft was rejected by his publishers and a furious Tolkien died thirty days later, after getting his head trapped in the mouth of his golf bag.

'If you can't stand the smell, get out of the toilet.'
Ancient proverb

In 2004 food scientist Heston Blumenthal invited celebrity friends round for a meal he considered his masterpiece. Bemused guests were fed what tasted to them like decidedly unspectacular food. Yet minutes later they were startled when they let out burps and farts of startling deliciousness. The sensation was said to be deeply disturbing and unsatisfying, however, and his guests set upon Blumenthal, eventually locking him in his garden until neighbours, alerted by his screams, called the police.

FARTING WORLD RECORDS

MOST VIBRANT FART

Italian opera singer Giambattista Tatonetti was famous in the 1970s not only for his girth but also for sending forth the most remarkably deep-rumbling farts. Indeed, after he set a world record in 1982 for singing so loudly he caused a Venetian vase to shatter, it was revealed he had not been singing at all, but had broken the glass with the resonant foghorn of his nether regions.

Before his action movie career, popular and handsome movie star Chuck Norris was best known for his farting antics on the 1970s comedy series Monk and Trench. Norris played a defrocked monk, nude and mentally deranged after being attacked with a garden rake by an elderly neighbour. His co-star, Colonel Trench (played by John Le Mesurier), was a curt upper-class British soldier who farted at the end of every line of dialogue. Each episode concluded with both of them being caught in some nefarious scheme, and soiling their pants. It was taken off the air after four episodes.

🏴 It's not widely known that in the famous roller skating scene in Charlie Chaplin's *Modern Times* (a shot for which he did over fifty takes), he was propelled by farts. For weeks beforehand he ate nothing but borlotti beans, and it is said that after this he wrote, produced, directed, scored and distributed all his own movies owing to no one else being able to share an edit suite with him.

WORDS OF WINDSDOM

'The best revenge is massive success. But the second best revenge is what I just did in my pants. Yeah, you smelt it yet? Ha! Now you did!'
FRANK SINATRA

🏴 The farting world's annual awards, the Farties, are held each year at the Hilton Hyde Park and attended by many of the country's most illustrious bottom trumpeters. Popular recipients of the Lifetime Achievement Award have included the late Richard Briers (for his pioneering 1990s reality TV series Colonoscopy Wars), and Joanna Trollope for her startlingly noxious sequence of novels about the life and loves of Karl J. Heinz.

The famous scene where Marilyn Monroe's dress blows up in *The Seven Year Itch* wasn't achieved with the use of a fan. In fact, a dietary note about Ms Monroe's food preferences failed to make it to the on-set caterers, which resulted in them serving food containing radishes to her dressing room – she was notoriously intolerant of root vegetables. The inevitable explosion happened in the middle of a take and the demure star carried it off so well that Billy Wilder decided to keep the shot in the final cut.

A little known film in the famous series, *Carry on Farting* (1979), was seen by many critics as one of the weakest. It is rarely shown on television because it ended up being only forty-nine minutes long after the BBFC made large cuts to a controversial subplot. In it, Kenneth Williams and Barbara Windsor harnessed the fart-energy of intensively farmed camels fed on rotting spinach to power a secret weapon (The Fartomax 2000) that they used to fight the Soviets alongside the Mujahaddin.

WORDS OF WINDSDOM

'A journey of a thousand miles begins with a simple step. Quickly! I've sharted!'
CONFUCIOUS

A British comedian of the 1950s, Tommy Tickles often made comic material out of his frequent gastric indelicacies – indeed, his cry of 'Whoops Mother' was adopted across the country for many years when someone let one fly. But in real life Tickles was a tragic figure, forced to avoid almost all social occasions because of his uncontrollable farting. Indeed, he lost out on his chance at movie stardom (the part of the 'milkman' in Marilyn Monroe's 1957 romance *Just Before Sundown*) due to farting loudly throughout the audition. Director Otto Preminger (a fan of Tickles) persisted for forty-seven takes, before giving up after Monroe had to be seen by a doctor because of breathing difficulties. Tickles was replaced by Norman Wisdom in the final film.

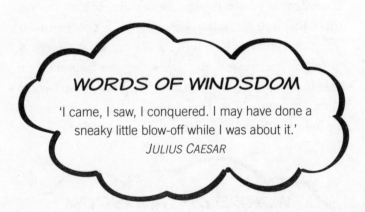

WORDS OF WINDSDOM

'I came, I saw, I conquered. I may have done a sneaky little blow-off while I was about it.'
JULIUS CAESAR

'If you fart in your bed, you must lie in it.'
Proverb

🌸 Burt Broccoli (aka Fart Man) was a superhero in the stable of short-lived British comics publisher Drat Comics. He was by far their most popular character, his adventures mostly taking part in the Second World War, where he foiled villains such as the Nazi general Wurst Burst, the Japanese Sushi Wooshi and Italian Captain Salami (whose depiction sailed close to the wind with Britain's obscenity laws). A 1976 film starring Malcolm McDowell featured him battling against a twenty-foot tall radioactive turd. It was widely ridiculed (many critics dubbing it 'Pooperman'), and was the last nail in the coffin for the struggling publisher.

'Empty bowels make the most noise.'
Proverb

🌸 Before the release of *A Grand Day Out*, British national treasures Wallace and Gromit were to be in a half-hour film called *A Gust for Life*. The plot featured intrepid but accident-prone Wallace developing a new form of universal laxative from concentrated prune juice. This early prototype, however, was not the heart-warming family fare we have come to know and love. Keen genre parodists from the start, Aardman Studios intended this as a vicious zombie satire of consumer society, stomach-churningly violent, with plasticine blood and flesh flying everywhere.

'He who farts last, farts longest.'
Proverb

BIG TRUMPS

Pit the most farty members of society against each other in a game of toxic proportions!

THE RULES

For those of you not at primary school during the eighties, here's how to play: shuffle the cards, then deal them out to each player, face down. Each player must then hold their cards so that they can only see the top card. The player to the left of the dealer starts by reading out a category from their top card (e.g. chance of meeting, score 55). The other players then announce their scores from the same category. The one with the highest score for that category wins, and that player collects all the top cards, including their own, and places them at the bottom of their pile. It is then their turn again to choose a category from the next card. If two or more cards share the same score for the category then all the cards are placed in the middle and the same player chooses again from their next card. The winner of the hand can then collect these cards from the middle at the end of the round. The person with all the cards at the end is the winner. OKAY?

THE STUDENT

The Student is enjoying her first term away from home, revelling in the freedom of doing exactly as she pleases, which includes breaking wind precisely wherever and whenever it suits her. She might not necessarily subsist on an exclusive diet of Pot Noodles as the cliché would have us believe, but she sure as hell hasn't taught herself to cook properly yet, so you can expect a belly full of highly spiced fast food and shots of those brightly coloured alcoholic drinks that no one on earth likes, but which eighteen- to twenty-one-year-olds force each other to consume. Combined with the appalling entitlement and arrogance of the young and happy, this makes the student a decidedly dangerous fart zone. Bloody students. Cut your hair and get a job, Trotsky!

Chance of meeting:	55
Outward respectability:	44
Dietary risk:	70
Social awareness:	59
Waft:	60
Stench:	69

THE FARMER

Spending his days surrounded by the gassy emissions of a multitude of animals has reduced the Farmer's social awareness to zero. Totally inured to barnyard odours, he is hardly able to detect them. There's a high risk of him letting out a guff he thinks is innocent and odourless (a noble gas, if you will), but which will wreak social havoc. Nevertheless, his diet is sturdy and healthy. Plus, how often do you meet a farmer, outside childhood? Hardly ever. You will only cross his path if you do so literally, by walking over his land thinking you had right of way. If you do meet, just engage him in conversation about any topics that spring to mind: foot and mouth disease, the criminal abuse of EU subsidies, the alarming level of depression and suicide in the farming community. You know, just light-hearted, everyday chitchat.

Chance of meeting:	50
Outward respectability:	64
Dietary risk:	45
Social awareness:	30
Waft:	73
Stench:	75

THE DEAD BODY

The thing about dead bodies is that they have absolutely no shame whatsoever. They're also completely rotten at conversation. Big on passive aggression. In fact, there's little to recommend them socially. Now, unless you are professionally obliged to do so, you are unlikely to run across many of them in your daily existence, I would hope. But should you encounter one, beware that besides growing fingernails and hair, the only other main activity people engage with after death is the occasional colossal blow-off. And expect that to be the one to end them all, so to speak. Phew! Excuse you! Someone open a bloody window! What do you mean, this morgue has no windows?

Chance of meeting: 10

Outward
  respectability: 0
Dietary risk: N/A
Social awareness: 0
Waft: 80
Stench: 89

THE OLD GUY NEXT DOOR

He seems like he means well, the Old Guy Next Door. But god knows what he eats because the guy stinks to high heaven. And you bump into him ALL THE TIME. You know it'd mean a lot to him if you bothered talking to the man. The one time you did have a chat with him, he became almost animated – talking about his former work. With animal skeletons. Or was it rocks? But your time is precious and you have so many enjoyable things you actually want to do. Oh well, he'll be dead soon anyway. Probably. Then you won't have to think about him.

Chance of meeting:	75
Outward respectability:	57
Dietary risk:	52
Social awareness:	55
Waft:	60
Stench:	71

THE CALL-CENTRE HIPPY

The Call-Centre Hippy is the only guy who hates himself more than you hate him. He wants to know whether you have received a good service today, and how you would rate it out of ten. Unfortunately, as one of the children of Gaia, he wants to live a pastoral existence of reciprocity, rather than in a row of blank cottages behind the Membury Services on the M4, near his dismal workplace – but in all likelihood, far away from you. He eats a medley of high-flatulence pulses and Middle Eastern salad dishes, just one of the reasons he's thoroughly unpopular at the call centre. It's not just the farting, or the fact he refuses to join in at five-a-side football. He's a gloomy sod.

Chance of meeting:	21
Outward respectability:	54
Dietary risk:	81
Social awareness:	46
Waft:	63
Stench:	76

THE OAP

The OAP is on the train on the way home from meeting up with her sister, who she intensely despises – but at least it's a familiar face. Once a week they meet up, in the café at Marks & Spencer. It's nice in there. She could get the bus but she doesn't feel comfortable on them any more – hardly a single white face. Oh dear. Let's steer away from her thoughts, then, and reflect that she hardly ever farts, but when you get older it's hard to maintain total control all the time. So there is a risk. And when it comes out it will reek, a peculiarly mouldy smell. I mean, this is quite a disgusting book, isn't it, when you think about it. Don't look at *me*. You're *reading* it.

Chance of meeting:	53
Outward respectability:	82
Dietary risk:	68
Social awareness:	70
Waft:	49
Stench:	74

THE WEIRD UNCLE

Everyone loves Uncle Rodney. He probably has some developmental issues, but it's never been properly diagnosed. I mean, he stands in the garden for up to six hours a day looking at the trees so there's clearly something up. But he's very dear – and extremely funny, although it's not always clear whether it's on purpose. He stinks a lot in general, because he has no inclination to wash, but he also refuses to eat anything except Asda microwaveable barbecue ribs. So he farts copiously and with visible pride.
They linger – they really linger. Maybe that's why he stands in the garden a lot.

Chance of meeting:	70
Outward respectability:	47
Dietary risk:	84
Social awareness:	40
Waft:	56
Stench:	82

THE AUTHOR

A creature of the shadows, one who snivels in darkness, the Author is a fugitive from taste and decency and society in general. He harboured dreams of being Tolstoy. Now he writes the copy that goes on adverts for thrush cream. Getting this fart book gig is very much the pinnacle of a career that would make other writers wake up screaming. He has invested the book's advance in multiple family-size bags of crisps from the 99p shop and bottles of 'DANGER – EXPLOSIVE!!!' chilli sauce, in which he dips those crisps while watching cabin-in-the-woods slasher movies, grinning. Hunched in his own filth, he waits for death.

Chance of meeting:	20
Outward respectability:	11
Dietary risk:	79
Social awareness:	57
Waft:	70
Stench:	80

THE JAZZ PIANIST

Life is jazz. Love is jazz. Work is jazz. The only thing that isn't jazz is . . . jazz? God damn, is there anyone you'd rather punch in the neck than the Jazz Pianist? A man who, moment by moment, pours his considerable skill into carefully preventing his music from being pleasant or listenable. He smokes coloured cigarettes and eats Lebanese food at three a.m. after he knocks off gigging for the night. When the waiters at the restaurant see him take a seat they utter a phrase that translates as 'the elephant who remembers everything still steps in his own turd'. Whatever that means. Bloody waiters.

Chance of meeting:	40
Outward respectability:	68
Dietary risk:	74
Social awareness:	60
Waft:	59
Stench:	75

THE LESBIAN PROFESSOR

If you ever accused her of farting (obviously you are far too scared of her ever to do so), she would likely explain that it is you who are in the wrong. That it is a paternalistic view of femininity that women should always be fragrant, and supports the current women-hating paradigm in our society. Well, yeah, I mean – but it still stinks. She lets fly frequently because she's past seventy now and also her girlfriend left her for the hottest female student on campus.

So, fuck the world, basically, is her standpoint.

I can see where she's coming from. Parp!

Chance of meeting:	49
Outward respectability:	79
Dietary risk:	55
Social awareness:	67
Waft:	56
Stench:	70

THE NERVOUS PHOTOCOPIER GUY

Oh god, he's always trying to catch your eye when you go to photocopy stuff. But you're always in a rush. Poor pathetic little chap, stuck at that tiny desk away from everyone else, facing the wall. And it's partly because of this loneliness that he feels he can get away with a fart now and then. Every time you go to the photocopier it seems to stink. You're not helping yourself make friends, mate! Especially with those curry peanuts you guzzle all day. You'd like to be nice to him, of course you would. But you're not going to. Because you can't be bothered.

Chance of meeting: 70
Outward respectability: 56
Dietary risk: 69
Social awareness: 49
Waft: 65
Stench: 63

SUSAN, WHO DOES SO MUCH MARVELLOUS WORK FOR CHARITY

Dear Susan, she thinks about other people all the time, and never thinks of herself. Silly girl. Silly, annoying girl. Everyone seems to be friends with her but no one seems to actually like her. Who needs to feel bad about themselves by putting up with a flipping do-gooder all the time? And she's vegan, which is a nightmare to cater for. Yes Susan. Yes, I know about factory farming conditions. Yes, it's awful, I agree. Sorry, did I splatter you with barbecue sauce? Oh dear. Was that new? It'll wash out.

Chance of meeting:	72
Outward respectability:	77
Dietary risk:	81
Social awareness:	75
Waft:	42
Stench:	61

THE SOCK COLLECTOR

Mad Dan McMullen, they call him. Started collecting socks in 1958 and now has over twenty thousand pairs. They had him in the *Guinness Book of World Records*. When he isn't buying more socks or cataloguing old ones, he's always in the library, hanging about outside the swimming baths or feeding the birds in the park (he's named them all – they're all called Stephanie). He stinks to high heaven – of socks, naturally, but also of his own unrestricted flow of bottom gas. There's always a slight suspicion he's about to get arrested for something deeply disturbing.
But he never does.
Funny old chap.

Chance of meeting:	**64**
Outward respectability:	**43**
Dietary risk:	**68**
Social awareness:	**52**
Waft:	**60**
Stench:	**73**

UNDERTAKER FREDDY

He's always in the village. At the post office.
Chatting away to the vicar, or a shopkeeper.
Everyone seems to think he's a marvellous chap,
old Freddy. But he makes your blood run cold.
The things he must have seen. All that time he's
spent alone with dead bodies. Do you think he
. . . no, no. Everyone says he's all right. Except
for the uncontrollable farting of course. But those
eyes. Might he have been tempted . . .
No, best not think about it.
Good old Freddy.
Sterling man.
Those rumours are
absolute hogwash
(shudder).

Chance of meeting: 67
Outward
  respectability: **80**
Dietary risk: **56**
Social awareness: 71
Waft: **54**
Stench: **61**

YOUR OLD MUSIC TEACHER

Oh god, you don't miss those days. Those days in the chilly music room after school. Stern Mr Steinberg in his loose-fitting cardies with their food stains, shuffling in his slippers. What gave those lessons their extra terror was that you could tell he was always just holding his anger in. He never let it out. Not once in five long years of you being persistently hopeless at the piano, and not trying to get better at the piano, and not giving a shit about the piano. However he did not control his rectum with quite such vigilance, and that cold room was often unpleasantly redolent of the cabbage-based cuisine of Schleswig-Holstein. These days you hear he's retired somewhere worryingly near to your parents' house.

Chance of meeting:	66
Outward respectability:	71
Dietary risk:	74
Social awareness:	60
Waft:	65
Stench:	62

THE MEDIEVAL PEASANT

He done brung in the wheat. So why then does his brother then make out that he is not done brung it in? He brung it in! His brother's got something funny in him head. Stupid brother. Sometimes the cows look at him funny. And he get up in middle of night and hit them with sticks. His bottom hurts. Medicine woman say eat more raw turnip then, but bottom hurt more. Angry bottom! He make burpy from it.

Chance of meeting: 0
Outward respectability: -4
Dietary risk: 76
Social awareness: 19
Waft: 70
Stench: 85

KORDOR OF LUBE

Kordor landed fifteen years ago, an emissary
from the planet Lube, from the Lube System.
In the Galaxy of Lube. He is supposed to bring
a message of peace and possible trade links
with these strange unscaly land-creatures. Both
planets have mineral deposits which would be
invaluable to the other and enormous prosperity
may come from it. But Kordor's taking it easy and

having a bit of a swim
first, and occasionally
giving a lonely sailor
the scare of his life.
He is, by nature,
a very lazy
alien man.
Naughty Kordor!

Chance of meeting: 23
Outward
  respectability: -465
Dietary risk: 70
Social awareness: 15
Waft: 79
Stench: 80

KHRUSHCHEV'S NEPHEW

Old Mr Karpovsky doesn't have many hobbies. Unless you can call getting arrested once or twice a week and shouting at the statues in Regent's Park, hobbies. He's Russian all right, as Russian as you like. He's also permanently drunk and highly garrulous, always talking. To trees mostly, and hedges and pigeons – also the occasional other tramp. In his native Russia he was renowned as a famous comedian. 'The Jolly Man of Vladivostock' was his nickname. He was expelled for bad comic timing. He is thirty-four years old.

Chance of meeting:	65
Outward respectability:	21
Dietary risk:	86
Social awareness:	33
Waft:	73
Stench:	79

THE FAILED BURGLAR

Carl was only a burglar for less than two hours. He knocked over a vase and the owner of the house came down. To his shame the guy refused to call the police, but gave him a stern talking to instead. Made him apologize. That broke him and he couldn't work after that. Now he's got the doctor to sign him off (not that he was working anyway) and he eats the damaged food his mum brings home from her job on the checkout at Iceland. Carl has little to do but gamble online and practise his farting.

Revolting little man.

Chance of meeting: 41
Outward respectability: 37
Dietary risk: 65
Social awareness: 52
Waft: 70
Stench: 73

BARBECUE DARREN

'You having a barbecue?' 'No, Darren.' 'Oh, I heard you were.' Sigh. 'So you are then. Can I come.' 'NO, Darren. It's always the same. You get drunk, eat all the food and then you . . . you fart. Copiously.' 'It's funny!' 'It *isn't* funny, Darren, it's bloody disgusting.' 'Come on, it's funny! You should loosen up mate!' 'I will *not* loosen up. I'm having Melissa's parents round for the first time tomorrow and I want to make an impression.' 'I can do impressions!' 'A good impression, Darren.' 'I do a very good Bobby Davro. I'll bring some bevies, see you around one, right?' (Sound of retreating farting noise.) 'Oh balls.'

Chance of meeting:	65
Outward respectability:	57
Dietary risk:	67
Social awareness:	41
Waft:	70
Stench:	72

ACKNOWLEDGEMENTS

Parts of this book first appeared in a different form in 1996 in the Journal of Medical Science, under the title 'Mice Are, Like, Really Stupid or Something', so for permission to reproduce it here I am indebted to the magazine's editor, Gregory 'Monkey Spamhole' Finbarr. I would also like to thank the late Penelope Fitzgerald for the loan of her canoe, Bob Dylan for all the soup, Ferdinand de Saussure, King Philip of Macedonia, bottles, green, a chair, another chair, Nijinsky (horse), Red Rum (rum), Harrison Birtwistle, Ray Winstone's infinite patience, Fatty Glossponse and her splendid sisters for a thrilling afternoon, water, roofs, bacteria, Katie Espiner, Hedy Lamarr, the Earl of Glasgow, lovely Kellie, Nijinsky (dancer), Mott the Hoople and St Agapetus of Pechersk.

MORE FROM BENET DONALD

Gardening in the Nude

Count Olav Karpovsky is haunted by the death of the young aristocrat he killed in a duel over the honour of his beloved Nastya. He ventures to Odessa and enters a monastery, seeking to expiate his unbearable guilt. But there he finds a wounded otter, which he nurses to health, and from there he disguises himself as a nun and moves to the wilderness of Wyoming. It is here that he has an epiphany: he is a total moron and has fucked things up. He takes to sleeping in a ditch, but gives it up after half an hour. Not an awful lot happens after that. Just lots of long sentences. I wouldn't buy it if I were you. Have you ever read Don deLillo's *White Noise*? Bloody marvellous. Buy that.

'A pioneering work, which any student of twentieth century politics would be foolish to ignore.'
Roy Jenkins

£7.99

Farm Stories #7: Happy Days

For young readers

Things have been going well on Happy Farm ever since Farmer Joe married Mary and she moved in, bringing her duck, Percy. However, trouble's afoot. Matilda the sheep and Abraham the grumpy cow have got into trouble with gambling debts, and Barry the Harsh Fucker is coming round with his boys. Soon all the farmyard animals are engaged in bloody tit-for-tat reprisals with a crew of Essex gangsters and mayhem erupts across the countryside. Will it all be sorted out before Penelope Pig has to judge the most delicious cake at the summer fete this weekend? No, it won't. Peaks in the middle and trails off a bit, to be honest. Probably not his best work.

'A book.' Gore Vidal

£5.99

The Weekly Planet

Kansas, 1952. When enthusiastic teenager James Sunday starts a newspaper in his bedroom called *The Weekly Planet*, little does he know that his world is about to be turned upside down. Into his life sweeps a glamorous cross-dressing Japanese pig wanker called Nick Mason, who is determined to use the newspaper to campaign for equal rights for cross-dressing professional pig wankers the world over. He does not succeed and both of them are beaten with sticks for a long time and forced to publically apologize, crying and with snot coming out of their noses. It gets quite boring after that, although there is a happy ending or whatever. Don't buy it. Get something good. Like *The Day of the Jackal.* That's a cracker.

'The worst.' Samuel L. Jackson

'Oh, Jesus.' Samuel L. Jackson

'I have to go now. Are you still recording me? Can you turn that thing off? Here, I want to turn it off myself. You, sir, are impolite.' Samuel L. Jackson

£7.99

The Life of Agrippa

A crucial figure in the history of the Roman Republic, Marcus Vipsanius Agrippa was a remarkably accomplished man, even among his many truly remarkable peers. A key general of Octavius (who became Emperor Augustus with his help), he not only helped rebuild Rome as a city of marble – helping design many of the Immortal City's most beautiful buildings – but was also an accomplished general who, with the decisive victory at the Battle of Actium, once and for all repelled the forces of Cleopatra and Marc Antony. He also transformed public health in Rome, rebuilding the aqueducts so that every Roman, irrespective of class, had access to baths and clean running water. In a magisterial survey of the statesman's career, Benet Donald provides not only a fascinating depiction of this crucial historical character, but a new way of looking at one of the most important empires in history.

'A work of towering scholarship. Rome will never seem the same for us again. A book for the ages.'
A. J. P. Taylor

£12.99

Jennifer

Once a gawky teenager mercilessly bullied in high school for her braces and bad posture, Jennifer Cole has emerged from university a proud major in quantum physics. Now she must undergo the biggest transformation of her life, from shy American student to a confident scientist at the CERN Large Hadron Collider, where after-hours experiments take her through a space portal to a distant planet where she commands a legion of fifty thousand bloodthirsty warriors. Will she find her way back before she succumbs to the charms of the brilliant and beautiful Arch-Mage Aggonath MacKellan? Yes, she will. He speaks exactly like Ian McKellen the actor, which is a bit of a turn-off for a straight woman who wants to get with a non-pompous man under fifty. Anyway, she shoots back through the timestream in time for dinner, which is lovely.

'I read and loved *The Time Machine* when I was a child.' Isaac Asimov

£7.99

ABOUT THE AUTHOR AND ILLUSTRATOR

Benet Donald

Benet Donald is a type of bowel disease found among the hill tribes of northern Borneo. Symptoms include intense throbbing, flashing lights and uncontrollable clenching. Commonly misdiagnosed as Claxton's Remediable Glutocorticosis, it can today be treated by over-the-counter medicine, although in some cultures there is still a crippling societal shame associated with the condition.

Tom Wharton

Tom Wharton is a 1997 romantic comedy starring Mira Sorvino and Stephen Dorff. Shelley is a hapless PA at a New York perfume company, who always seems to be the bridesmaid at her friends' weddings. But her life is turned upside down when she inherits an abandoned goldmine on an Indian reservation and is thrown into the hands of a charismatic attorney who suffers from face blindness.